Irene,

May the morning be
of each new day shine
on your path through this to
May the Divine presence illuminate
your heart with a love that surpasses
every boundary, overcomes any obstacle,
and lasts throughout eternity. May hope
be the beauty that drives
you forward!

Peace Be With
You,

The Mourning Light

R. B. Craven

ISBN 978-1-0980-5630-8 (paperback)
ISBN 978-1-0980-7998-7 (hardcover)
ISBN 978-1-0980-5631-5 (digital)

Christian Faith Publishing, Inc.
832 Park Avenue
Meadville, PA 16335
www.christianfaithpublishing.com

[Scripture quotations are from the] *Revised Standard Version of the Bible—Second Catholic Edition (Ignatius Edition)*, copyright © 2006 National Council of the Churches of Christ in the United States of America. Used by permission. All rights reserved.

Printed in the United States of America

Endorsements

No more beautiful words have ever been spoken. The poem that spoke to me the most was: "I Must Forgive". Even though we have the same core belief of LOVE, we approach it from different paths. You are such a beautiful soul and you are my soul sister and I am honored that you would share these loving words with me. Keep writing. It's obvious that you were given Divine intervention to write...so keep writing these beautiful words of Love. Namaste.

—Dorothy Bonk

I laughed, I cried, I was blessed. Thank you for sharing!

—Jody Ackerman
Carbon County Senior Care

Mourning Light is the poetry of a hurting soul, held by God.

—Linda Picchioni

R. B. Craven has touched my heart deeply with her poems, her stories, and most of all her soul. She has lived deeply a life with God and her soul reflects the beauty of starlight from Heaven. C. S. Lewis once said that friendship is born when another person shares a greatest joy or greatest burden that happens to be the very same joy or burden we bear. With the joys and burdens Craven has shared in *The Mourning Light*, you will likely find as I have, that in reading this book, we have made a new friend.

—Ed Nilson

The Mourning Light by R. B. Craven is truly a gift crafted from insight, thoughtfulness and care. This work is a wonderful and perfect blend of spiritual inspiration that promotes love and healing by weaving the author's original verse with traditional scripture and quotations. Craven asks and answers tough life questions with her own distinctive and gentle voice.

—Terri Malucci
Author and Artist

In her new book, *The Mourning Light*, R. B. Craven skillfully weaves a tapestry of poetry and prose to lead the reader on a beautiful and sensitive journey through the wilderness of the losses of loved ones. From the clever title to germane citations from Sacred Scripture, Saints and Fathers of the Church, Craven provides the "Balm of Gilead" to heal our grieving souls. In writing The Mourning Light, Craven worked through her grief. Her book should help anyone of us who suffers loss and grief.

—Rev. Paul R. Cook, MD, MHA
Deacon, Diocese of Great Falls-Billings

This is a beautiful book to accompany anyone who is on the journey of trying to heal from the loss of a loved one or who is trying to help someone else to heal. Ruth shares the stories of her own grief, the stories of family and friends, and all the research that she did on how to come through grief to a place of joy again. Her stories are interspersed with the most beautiful poems that will touch your heart with their ability to capture the depth of the feelings of loss and the hope that we have through our Faith in God. Everyone who reads this book will be touched by a gift of love—the love of human beings for each other and the love that God has for all of us. This is a book to be read again and again.

—Mary Cook, Red Lodge, MT

I went through your manuscript and found it to be very thoughtful and inspiring. You have brought out many inspiring insights about life and death. Your faith filled experience that you have shared here makes one to realize how important it is to build a loving relationship with God and with one another. We cannot isolate ourselves from the realities of our life. We need to face them with faith and courage.

Secondly, it is always difficult to console someone who is grieving because we do not know the depth and intensity of their pain and sorrow at the loss of their loved ones. I really appreciate the way you brought out different phases of life and sorrow of our journey here on earth. I am sure these thoughts will inspire all to cope up with their loss. Quotes from Bible and saints add a great meaning to your insights here.

Good job. Well done.

God bless.

—Fr. Navil

Only in the darkness can we ever see the light.
The miracles of strength and truth continue burning bright.
Without the pains and hurts of sorrow,
Strength can't overcome the morrow,
But when we win the battles fought, we
find the peacefulness we sought.

This book is dedicated to my best friend, my rock, my beautiful mother, Rosa Garrido Blas, who continues to live in the hearts of those whose lives were touched by her gracious care. Her unfailing and never-ending love encouraged me to write. It is through her purity of heart that my life has been built upon a strong foundation of faith, hope, and love. Her perseverance in faith, her constant hope, and her unconditional love was the inspiration in which these writings blossomed. This book is the fruit of her faith in me.

Foreword

Those who know Ruth Craven know that she lives to love others and to serve others, to use what she has been given to share with others. And so it is that her *The Mourning Light* is a testament to those purposes. In a medley of poems, prayers, meditations, accounts of personal experiences, as well as quotations from saints and holy scripture, she seeks to lead others through the difficulties of life—the sadness, the grief that comes with loss. "Only in the darkness can we ever see the light," is how this work begins, and it is indeed a voyage from darkness into light. She wishes to be a lantern to others, to help others get through the darkness to the light, through the night to the dawn.

How to deal with the death of a family member, a friend, a beloved spouse, and, perhaps most difficult of all, the loss of a child, she has experienced all of these.

Writing these poems, prayers, and meditations helped her get through these times, and so may they be of use to her readers, as they were meant to be. Ruth's love of God and love of others, her faith, her hope, her devotion to her church shine throughout. Heartfelt expression and honest portrayal of feelings may inspire the reader to follow along. How helpful it is to have a lantern in the dark! To know that someone has cared enough not merely to get through the darkness but to help others get to the light. And not with boasting or embellishing, but with a serious look into the stages of grief and with humbleness and sincerity that come with true feeling and honest meditation.

May the readers find their consolation and their way by following these footsteps.

Roberta Simone
Professor of Literature, Emeritus
Grand Valley State University, Michigan

11

Part 1

Life is so short. Our time on earth is only an instant in the scope of eternity, and in that short moment, we make such an impact on everything that surrounds us. Life, like a twenty-four-hour cycle, can be reflected in the process of a day. The sun shines, and we live in the warmth and the light of its glow. The sun sets, and we search for rest and safety in the loss of light and the coolness of night. We find rest, and then we are refreshed to begin again. Life is the daytime, death is the nighttime, and dawn is the hope of life eternal.

I wrote these poems with love for family and friends who were grieving for a loved one who passed away, and through my own grief, writing them helped me accept the loss and led me to a place of acceptance and of healing. As I researched and wrote, I embarked on a journey of self-discovery and a deeper spirituality. Healing comes with faith, and this faith opens the eyes to the dawn, the new light, the beginning of a new day. I hope my experiences, my thoughts, my words, and my research inspire healing and help you through the process of mourning. I hope you can see the dawning of each new day.

> For God alone my soul waits in silence, for my hope is from Him. (Psalms 62:5)
>
> May Christ support us all the day long, 'til the shadows lengthen, and the evening comes, and the busy world is hushed, and the fever of life is over and our work is done. Then in His mercy may He give us a safe lodging and holy rest and peace at the last. (John Henry Cardinal Newman)

Mourning Light

FAITH will reveal God's Mourning Light
When shadows stir within the night.
In this dark and gloomy hour,
Sadness steals away my power.
Will ever the pain inside me heal?
When will time ease what I feel?
How can life just continue on
When a part of my life is forever gone?
I wonder why they had to leave
And why I'm left to mourn and grieve?
My sorrow leads my thoughts to roam,
But I feel my loved one's safely home.
So, I'll hope in God, who is the Way;
My dearly departed has found the new day.
And as my hope brings dawn in sight,
FAITH will reveal God's Mourning Light.

When Grief Strikes

When someone you love dies suddenly,
Grief strikes swift and painfully.
The sadness can consume the hole
Left from the loss of a beautiful soul.
God's healing power will conquer all.
He'll pick you up after this fall;
Just ask, and you'll receive His Grace.
It may be a smile from a gentle face,
It may be a hug from a caring friend,
Or to know there's a beginning after the end.
The healing will come at its own pace;
Death and grief will hide their face.
Then peace will come, and you'll be fine;
When mourning ends, the light will shine.

Changed

There was a change in my life today:
Gloom filled the skies and darkness came to play.
The sadness of my heart caused me to quickly age.
My aching soul was dying, and my red eyes burned with rage.
I lost one of my beloved to a state of permanent rest,
But it's hard to hear condolences and believe that God knows best.
Why do we have to hurt this much and suffer through this strife
When time just ends and we lose the ones we love so much in life?
I think I'm going crazy with all this rage inside.
My sorrow and my anger are confusing and collide.
Is God going to heal me or bring my heart to peace?
Will God somehow teach me to let go and to release?
Will there be a change in my life someday,
When the gloom disappears and the clouds roll away?
Will the light of the Son penetrate my aching heart?
And will my hope in Him renew me to a new and loving start?

There is no experience quite like losing someone we love to death. Separation is always difficult, especially when we know it is permanent. I've lost a number of people I've cared for from natural death, by accident, even those who experienced so much pain in life who decided they could no longer go on living. It didn't matter how I'd lost them; it only mattered that I did lose them. Sadness has a way of gripping your heart, but its grip loosens over time because of love and everything involved in loving. Love is the connection between souls. When life no longer flows through one's physical body, love still exists between the two individuals. This unconditional love prompts healing.

Do not look forward in fear to the changes
in life; rather, look to them with full hope that
as they arise, God, whose very own you are, will
lead you safely through all things; and when you
cannot stand it, God will carry you in His arms.

Do not fear what may happen tomorrow; the same understanding Father who cares for you today will take care of you then and every day.

He will either shield you from suffering or will give you unfailing strength to bear it. Be at peace, and put aside all anxious thoughts and imaginations. (St. Francis de Sales)

You arouse us so that praising you may bring us joy, because you have made us and drawn us to yourself, and our heart is unquiet until it rests in you. (St. Augustine of Hippo)

It was a beautiful day. The sun was shining, the birds were singing, and it was so peaceful, seemingly perfect. It was Memorial Day of 1995, and my father wanted those of us staying home to help him landscape our family property. My family always worked in unison, and when we worked together on occasions such as this, our bond to one another strengthened. Our family property was quite secluded at that time, and it was raw land. We'd built a work shack there for whenever we went to clean and work the land. That day we were clearing things, and it was approaching lunchtime. My mother and I barbecued beef and prepared lunch. The family gathered, and we enjoyed a wonderful meal together, talking, sharing, and laughing a lot. After lunch, we went back to work, and it felt wonderful being in this peaceful place building a sanctuary together. It was one of those times when you feel accomplished and happy because of the progress you've made. My mother and I gathered the dishes, the leftover food, and the trash to take home. As evening came, the family gathered everything up to go back home and rest. This was one of my fondest memories with my family.

My father was retired, so the following day, on a Tuesday, he wanted to go back and work on the property. I was babysitting, and my mother was going to run errands with one of my sisters in the afternoon, so we stayed home. It was a very hot day, so my mother was a little concerned about my father going up to the land alone.

My other sister, Helen, decided to go up and work on her property, which was just a couple of lots away from where my father was working. My mother prepared my father's favorite dish, fried reef fish with white rice and vegetables, for lunch and asked my sister to bring it up to him. She brought the food up, and they ate a nice lunch together. My sister went to her property to start working, but something was bothering her. My dad was sweating profusely after lunch, so she decided to go back and check on him.

About an hour after my sister left the house with the food, my cousins were outside frantically yelling for my mom. "Auntie Chai, you need to go to the ranch because Uncle Frank passed out! We've called for an ambulance, and we'll wait here for them, then bring them up to the property." My brother Ben just came home, and my friend Pete had come to visit, so we all jumped in Pete's truck and headed up to the property. As we drove up, we saw my sister giving my father CPR. Ben and I jumped out and took over from her. It was so difficult to stay calm, breathe for my dad, and hear my brother counting as he pumped Dad's heart. My sister, exhausted, tried to catch her breath and remained composed as she began to explain to my mom what had happened. She had found him faced down when she came back to check on him. She somehow was able to get help and began CPR. My cousins called 911, then came to get us. Ben and I continued CPR. I could hear the dread in her voice as she explained the events. Every time I blew into my dad's mouth, I hoped there was still a chance that he wasn't gone. My brother urged us not to give up and to continue CPR until the ambulance came. We didn't stop. It seemed as though the medics were taking forever to get there, and we were getting tired, even though the three of us were switching on and off. The ambulance finally came, and the medics took over. Mom and Ben rode in my father's pickup, and they followed the ambulance to the hospital. We all were supposed to meet her there.

I'm the youngest of eight, so, instead of rushing to the hospital, I called all of my other brothers and sisters to tell them what was happening. I couldn't get ahold of my brother Dave, so instead of going straight to the hospital, I asked Pete to take me to Dave's house so I could tell him what had happened. I didn't want to face what I already knew. My father had passed away. I couldn't understand why this would happen so suddenly. He was so strong and vibrant. I went to Dave's to pretend that Dad was going to be all right, even if I knew in my heart what I was going to face. As it turned out, Dave wasn't home, and I had wasted the trip. When I finally got to the hospital, my mother scolded me and asked me why it took me so long to get there. Ben told me afterward that he was crying while he was driving and that Mom was so strong. She kept him focused enough to drive safely. My siblings and I had always seen my mom as a rock. I was sorry for what I had done. I was twenty-five. I should have known that my mom needed me, needed all of her children around her and safely with her. She told me that my dad had had a massive heart attack and had died instantly. He was gone. Crying, I apologized to her, and she took me in her arms and held me. I told her I didn't want to know that Dad was dead.

In our custom, we call all our close relatives when someone passes. They come to the hospital and gather for the viewing of the body. When the family is all there, we pray together. When we are done, the coroner takes the body away for preparation, and the family begins to grieve. My family is mostly Catholic, and our tradition, culturally and religiously, requires us to have a nine-day rosary, a viewing (traditionally a wake throughout the night before the funeral), the closing of the casket before the funeral mass, then the rite of Christian burial. I was so grateful for this tradition. All of our extended family, uncles, aunts, cousins, nieces, nephews, and friends came each day to pray for my father and my family. Every day we would prepare food, and people would come to help set up for the evening prayers. We'd prepare the coffee, drinks, and snacks, set up chairs and the tables for the food people would bring, and then clean up. During this preparation, the people who came to help usually shared some of their experiences with our dad with us. It was really nice to hear and to know how my father had bonded with others and made a difference in the lives he touched.

We would also say a noon rosary. This always comforted me because it turned my mind to God and to life after death. My sisters and I would take turns leading this afternoon prayer, and it brought us closer each time. Whenever it was my turn to lead, I felt more comfort in my soul. I guess it was because I was focused on God and the prayer, which gave me more faith. It also gave me a glimpse of the beyond, since we meditate on the life, death, and resurrection of Jesus, while asking the Blessed Mother to pray for us.

The nightly gathering of people was a great show of love and support. Every person that had been touched by my father came and shared their personal stories of this wonderful man. It isn't like a memorial service where people stand in front of a room and share experiences; it was much more intimate. When my family would greet people, they always told us how they knew my dad. I found out more about my father after he died than when he was alive. People told me things about him as a child or as a teenager or accomplishments he'd made at work or how he had helped them when they needed help. I learned of his integrity, generosity, and that he was highly regarded by friends and relatives alike. He had so many friends and was dearly loved. I discovered the many different hats my father had worn, and I am extremely grateful that he was my dad.

The nightly rosaries kept my family very busy and especially helped my mom. We would prepare drinks and refreshments for the people who attended the rosary and prepare the table for those who brought food to share. The work of preparing every night kept our emotions under control. The reminiscing, the stories, and the company helped to keep him present, and as the people gathered in prayer, my faith was constantly fed by the faithful, because, one after another, they would say my dad was with God now, and I believed them.

Sometimes people would say that my dad's spirit visited them. I believed this too but wondered why he wouldn't visit me. Then one night, I dreamed of him. It was not a very nice or peaceful dream. He came up to me while my brothers and sisters were arguing about who was going to take care of my mom and said to me, "You'd better take care of your mother!" Then he left. Although I knew I was asleep and that my father was gone, I also knew my father was serious. I stayed with my mom and helped her manage her finances, which my father had always done, until she learned how to take care of them herself. I slept with her for an entire year after that and didn't want to leave her side until she was ready. She was always so strong though that I think maybe I stayed with her more for myself than for her.

My father's funeral was a very emotional time. There were over one thousand people present that day to pay their respects to a man who had in some way touched their lives. What a tremendous impact my father had on those with whom he came in contact. It was beautiful to see how much he was loved in life. But I hated seeing my dad's body in the coffin. This lifeless man did not look anything like my handsome, vibrant father, so I knew right then and there that he was with God and that his spirit lived on in heaven. The viewing was held at our house, and the coffin was in the living room. My family stood or sat by my father's body in a receiving line and heard the condolences of those who came, most of whom had been attending the nightly prayers. Dave, my fifth oldest sibling, was showing me the mass program. On its back was this poem by an unknown author:

Safely Home

I am home in heaven, dear ones;
Oh so happy and so bright!
There is perfect joy and beauty
In this everlasting light.
All the pain and grief is over,
Every restless tossing passed;
I am now at peace forever,
Safely home in heaven at last.
Did you wonder how I so calmly
Trod the valley of the shade?
Oh, but Jesus' love illumined
Every dark and fearful glade.
And he came himself to meet me
In that way so hard to tread;
And with Jesus' arm to lean on,
Could I have one doubt or dread?
Then you must not grieve so sorely,

For I love you dearly still;
Try to look beyond earth's shadows,
Pray to trust our Father's will.
There is work still waiting for you,
So, you must not idly stand;
Do it now, while life remains,
You shall rest in Jesus' land.
When that work is all completed,
He will gently call you home;
Oh, the rapture of that meeting,
Oh, the joy to see you come!

I read it and started to weep. I don't remember if my tears were of joy or sorrow, maybe both, but my heart was full of love. When it was time to close the coffin, a few of my cousins started to sing "Wind Beneath My Wings," and as we said our goodbyes, my family held on to one another, all of us heartbroken, and cried. The casket was closed, and we convoyed to the church, following the hearse for the mass, then to the cemetery where we buried his body. After the funeral, the grief hit us a little harder. I mourned, I cried, I wrote, and then I began to heal. It's been over twenty years since my father passed away, but I can still feel him, and I know he is always present in my life. I can close my eyes and see his face clearly. I can still hear his voice teaching me long division, giving me advice, or singing with my mom while sitting in a chair under the moonlight. I pray for him, and I'm confident he prays for us. God has imprinted my dad's love in the fabric of our lives, and this weaving of a patchwork quilt of love and memories will never tear. When I look back, many times the two days merge together in my mind, that wonderful day with family and then the dreaded one that followed. I think my mind copes with it by balancing the good and bad moments. I believe this is God's doing. He's just reminding me to focus on love. My siblings and my mother remember this time differently. Our perceptions vary from one person to another, and the trauma of the event affected us in different ways. We healed separately, but our bond as a family strengthened as a whole.

Whether a person believes in life after death or not, the love exchanged between two people remains. The ripples of that love affect each life it touches, and those feelings and effects cannot be reversed. Our lives are changed because of love, the love of family, friends, acquaintances, and even strangers. The death of my father, and the experience with the community that loved him, gave me another goal in life: to love. Love will never die. "Love is as strong as death" (Song of Solomon 8:6).

In the end, we will be judged by love alone. (St. John of the Cross)

Go out into the world today and love the people you meet. Let your presence light new light in the hearts of people.(St. Teresa of Calcutta)

Thinking of You

Sitting here just thinking of you,
I watch the clouds move slowly by.
I know you're out there somewhere
In that beautiful, big, blue sky.
Your spirit fills the air around me
Below, beside, above.
We'll meet someday in paradise,
But for now, I'll breathe into your love.
I don't really think life ever ends.
It just transcends this realm of touch.
So know, my beautiful father,
That I still love you very much.

Home Today

A cherub took me home today.
She appeared and said, "Be merry."
'Cause she was there to guide my way,

Yet I was a little weary.
She said, "It's time to leave this place.
Our Father needs you elsewhere."
But I saw you crying wholeheartedly
And wanted to stay near.
I have to be obedient,
So say goodbye to me.
It's time to start your life anew.
I hereby set you free.
Thank you for your love for me,
But now it's time to part.
I'll watch you always from where I am
And pray God heals your heart.

Faith, Hope, Love

Faith gets you through the storms.
Hope lets you see the rainbow and the promises of His covenant.
Love brings you to peaceful waters.
May faith, hope, and love find you.

> So faith, hope and love abide, these three;
> but the greatest of these is love. (1 Corinthians
> 13:13)

Trumpets Sounded

Trumpets sounded when I arrived.
The angels greeted me in heaven above.
Remember me in the future
With laughter, joy, and love.
Rejoice, because God forgave me
For whatever offense I've made.
I told him I was sorry,
And He said His Son had paid.
He said He loves us so much

And His Son had suffered so.
He saved us with His ransom,
And through Jesus's cross, we'd grow.
You have to share God's love now
And prepare for His great coming.
Have faith in all He's taught us
And continue to do His bidding.

Spirit Voice

My life has always been open
With blessings raining down.
The voices of the spirit world
Have never made a sound,
But now I'm asking you to listen,
To open up an ear,
For my spirit voice is speaking
If you only choose to hear.
Be comforted in what life holds,
For Our Father has a plan.
Have faith in all His promises
He made when He was man.
We rise to meet our Maker
The moment our breath ends,
So live your life with acts of love
And be quick to make amends.

I lift up my eyes to the hills. From where does my help come? My help comes from the Lord, who made heaven and earth.

The Lord will keep you from all evil; he will keep your life. The Lord will keep your going out and your coming in from this time forth and forevermore.

(Psalms 121:1-2, 7–8)

My Earthen Beauty

From the heavens, I clearly see
The earthen beauty below.
The colors blend in harmonious splendor
More glorious than a rainbow.
The greens of grass and trees and plants
With all their different hues
Accentuating vivid colors—
The yellows, reds and blues.
As I watched the splendor down below,
A spectacular sight caught my eye.
It filled my soul with love and care
As I looked down in awe from the sky.
Like a little island in the sun
Surrounded by a sparkling sea,
I saw how God had blessed my life
With the place that was home to me.
A wonderful feeling came into my soul
Seeing family and friends gathering 'round,
Laughing and sharing about their times spent with me.
I know their love has no bounds.
My life there on earth was well lived and sweet.
God blessed me with all that has passed.
However, nothing compares with the peace I feel now;
I'm at home in heaven at last.

My mother's life was changed drastically after my father's death, because they had been together for so long. He was twenty-five and she was sixteen when they married in 1950. In that era and in our culture, marriage at sixteen was common. They were married for forty-five years, so they grew together and learned about life with each other. They were never physically separated for any long time. She never remarried and still remembered, with perfect clarity, her life with him. Some specific moments made her smile, some made her mad, and others made her sad. She had to adapt to a lot of different responsibilities after my dad died, because he took care of most of the technical things, such as paying bills and managing finances. She also had to deal with our grief. My mom had such a deep faith in God and a very healthy understanding of death that carried me and held me up through that time. I'm grateful for all her strength. I asked her, years later, how she remained strong. She said that she had to be strong for us. She was still taking care of her kids! She also said that we all belong to God, and we just have to know that God will take care of us through the hard times.

Several aunts, uncles, and cousins had passed away before my dad did, and I've had many experiences of loss in my life that affected its course, but the loss of my father was the first experience that changed my view of life itself. I came to realize just how short and quick it can be. I started questioning things, such as the purpose for which we are here. I was angry because I truly believed my father was too young to die and that we still needed him. He was only seventy years old at the time of the heart attack. I felt guilty because he hadn't seen me succeed in my career, and he would never get to meet my children, because I had waited too long to have any. I would contemplate in solitary hours the "what ifs" and "should've dones," and then I'd look up and feel his presence, hoping he could hear me and feel my love. I started researching grief so that I could understand my feelings better. I hoped I wasn't going crazy. I discovered that grief takes time to go through. It also goes through many stages.

I'm not sure if my brothers and sisters went through the same thing I went through, because we all had viewed our father differently, but I know it was different for my mother. For all of us, our lives changed dramatically after his death. The head of our family was gone. Through this life-changing ordeal, I clung to the emotions I felt when he died. My emotions were raw, and it was hard to control it. Many times, I was overwhelmed with sadness, anger, and self-pity, and during that time, I wasn't a patient or friendly person. I didn't really know how to cope with his death, because a lot of those feelings were new. They were foreign, and I was in unknown territory.

Now, I believe there are angels everywhere! I see them in the faces of all my family and friends. These are my protectors, my confidants, my reasons to have faith in love and goodness. I hope I can be as much a force to those who know me. I started writing to my mom to let her know how I felt about her while she was still alive. I appreciate my mother more now than ever and always want her to know that her sacrifices were never made in vain.

The Gardener

We are the garden you've been given to tend,
From the time we were born until the end.
You tend us with love and comfort each day.
With a firm and caring hand, you guided our way.
Though each of our colors differ in the light,
Our roots remain strong and our stems upright.
We are the garden you've tended since birth.
Watch our beauty spread though the earth.
Thanks to the Gardener.

A True Reflection

You are a true reflection of our Holy Father's love.
Like Jesus gave his life to save God's children,
You've devoted every day of your life to the care of your children;
You give us comfort when we cry;
You give us hope when faith is hidden.
You carry us when we fall and force us to
walk the paths that we have chosen;
You make us aware that our burdens are light
by bearing the weight of our failures.
You restore our spirits, and you do it through love.
Thank you.

Because of You

You taught me how to take my time
And live life day by day.

I learned to see the best in things,
And it's helped along the way.
You said that every trial is solved.
I know this to be true,
For with this knowledge, I strive for dreams
And do what I can do.
"Always try with your very best,"
I've heard you often say.
"At least you'll learn from your mistakes
And find another way."
I make each step without a doubt
Seeing life with a bright point of view,
I take my time to live each day,
And it's all because of you.

A Star

God blessed me with a star
that shined through every night.
It sparkled in the darkness
And guided me with light.
My star revealed a lot of things
Which ignited ideas in me.
Now I can share my thoughts and views
Through gifted creativity.
I've always looked up to my star,
Although you didn't know.
My guiding light, my Northern Star
Is none other, Mom, than you.

Enjoy the Ride

You held my hand when I was scared and told me not to worry.
You said to take it easy in life and never rush or hurry.
In life, you never fret too much; you just enjoy the ride,
Never being one to step on toes or hide behind your pride.

You taught me how to love the arts and appreciate life's beauty.
You also taught me how to dance and really shake my booty.
I'm older now, with a busy life, but one thing is crystal clear.
I love you dearly, Mama, so know I'll *always* care,
And you're always in my prayers.

Your Love for Us

How beautiful your love for us,
So pure and so true,
No strings attached or fear to fall,
Your love is unconditional.
It's shaped each one of us in care
And taught us how to give and share.
Thank you, Mom, for the seeds you sow.
Our lives continue to thrive and grow.

We know that death is a part of the natural cycle of life, but we don't deal with the death of our loved ones enough to get used to the feelings of loss. In my research, I found that there are seven stages of grief:

- Shock & Denial: The natural reaction to losing a loved one is numbed disbelief. Shock provides emotional protection from being overwhelmed by the news. We may deny, at some level, that the loss has taken place in order to avoid the pain. This stage may last a few moments or for weeks.
- Pain & Guilt: As the shock wears off, a feeling of unbelievable pain and suffering replaces it. It may seem unbearable and excruciating, but it is important that you experience the pain fully, and not hide it, escape it or avoid it with drugs and/or alcohol. Guilt or remorse over things you did or didn't do with your loved one may occur. Life feels chaotic and scary during this phase.
- Anger & Bargaining: It is natural to feel anger when you are in pain. You may want to blame someone or something for causing that pain (even if the person is gone). Frustration

may occur and you may want to lash out at those around you because it's convenient. Be careful with this and try to have self-control because acting out of anger and blame can permanently damage a relationship with someone who is really trying to help you by being there. You may be angry at yourself for not being able to "save" your loved one. You must come to terms that no one is to blame.

In this stage, we tend to ask the question "why?" Why is this happening to me? Why did this happen? Why couldn't it have been me instead? and so on. You might even try to bargain with God as a way to escape the pain. For instance, "I will go to church every day if you just bring him back." Again, I stress that this is a natural feeling.

- Depression, Reflection, Loneliness: When you finally realize the truth of your loss, you are depressed. Those around you may try to encourage you to go on with your life, but a period of sad reflection may consume you. You may feel dull, still angry underneath, but this is a normal stage of grief. Your friends and family may mean well by trying to talk you out of your sullenness, but that is not helpful during this stage. You may withdraw from your usual social contacts or isolate yourself on purpose.

During your isolation, you may reflect on your relationship or on the life of your loved one. While you reminisce, feelings of emptiness and despair may accompany your reflection.

- The Upward Turn: During this period, you may start feeling a little more calm and controlled. You start to adjust your life to living without your loved one and your physical symptoms start to decrease. Your depression begins to ease.
- Reconstruction & Working Through: As you become stronger, you become more functional. The adjustment to living without your loved one becomes easier and you start

to think about things that are more practical. The pain of your loss does not hinder your mind anymore.

- Acceptance & Hope: This is when you learn to accept and deal with the reality of your situation. Acceptance doesn't necessarily mean that happiness is instant, but it does bring you forward and closer to it. This is when you are at peace with the loss and you start to have hope for the future.

Elisabeth Kubler-Ross wrote this *On Death and Dying*, a book that has become well known on these stages of grief.

It helped a little to know that the feelings I was going through would eventually end and that they were common among people who have lost dear ones. We are all different, so we grieve and heal differently. I turned to God and started reading the Bible. I prayed more and started relating to those words in the Bible that I could never understand before; then, I started writing—writing letters to God, writing poems, writing honest thoughts and feelings, just writing. I embraced my hurt close to me so that I could express it with pen and paper. My sorrow became a transformation in my life, and I appreciate all I have now. You can see the stages of grief I was in by the tones of my poems. I released a lot of anger. My writing warded off my depression, and then I started to understand. And with that understanding came hope. I read my journal entries, and I noticed the change in my thinking patterns. I was healing, and in the process, I found new hope, deeper faith, and greater love.

As you go through the same stages, I encourage you to express your emotions in ways in which you are comfortable. There is no wrong way to grieve, and there is no wrong way to heal. Writing has helped me, because I can look back and see my progress. It has been a gift that gives me grace. Journalizing, painting, sculpting, building, praying, and speaking are all positive and helpful. There are many venues in which you can express your thoughts and emotions, both privately and publicly. Personally, I've had days when I needed to pray just to get out of bed or to eat. Dealing with our grief is hard, and when we try to bottle it up, a flood comes later. Understand that going through the motion of your emotions will bring healing, hope, and faith. You are not alone.

> Blessed are those who mourn, for they shall
> be comforted. (Matthew 5:4)

My experiences with death have transformed my thinking of life. This transformation led me to the Bible and has given me a new understanding of what is important. For me, Matthew 5:4 was true the instant I read it, because I was comforted when I mourned. One day, I prayed for comfort and for clarity, and God answered me. A great feeling of peace came over me, and my view of death changed. I now try to keep my heart in heaven and live to love my neighbor. I strive to live beyond myself, and God has spoken to my soul when I chose to listen. Who better to ask for strength, healing, and guidance than the One that knows our souls most intimately? Many people turn to what they are familiar with to find comfort. I turned to God and found love in faith and the community of the church, and they comforted me. I know now that I will never be alone, and that if I look close enough, I can see the face of God in those around me who share in my sorrow and who share my joy. It is one image of love.

Come to Me

Come to me you weary souls; lay your burdens on my cross.
When your strength comes back to full,
you'll find that you were never lost.
Wrap your pain and send it to me—that will be your part.
I will guide you through each day and heal your broken heart.
I called my child home to me because his tasks were done.
I wanted him in paradise to dwell with us, the three in one.
You may not understand my plan, but believe that I know best.
Your loved one is at home now and peacefully at rest.
For every hurt, a lesson hides, so find it through the pain.
Your reward is great in heaven for the hope and faith you gain.

> Trust in Him at all times, O people; pour out your heart before Him; God is a refuge for us. (Psalms 62:8)

Your Loss

Looking down from high above, hoping you'll be fine,
I see the grief that you must feel, the worry on your mind.
I sit and ponder the outcome of a person who used to be
Full of faith and hope and love, a pillar of strength and security.
But when life parted us to separate ways, your goals parted too,
And now you pass each single day without a different view.
The glow that once had shown from your
eyes has become a shadow of gloom.
Misled because of Satan's lies. Its darkness may become your doom.
I know you think you've lost my love, and it's leading to despair.
I see your heart is grief's abode. You've lost your will to care.
Your values are hidden behind a wall…
your mourning leaves you broken.
Please listen closely to my call so the door of love will open.
You need to know that love will heal, and
mourning will come to an end.
Just lift your eyes so that God is revealed.
Let the grace of His Spirit descend.

> This is my comfort in my affliction that your promise gives me life. (Psalms 119:50)

Before I Bid Goodbye

I wish you safe, I wish you well.
I'll miss you always though words may fail,
And so before I bid goodbye,
My love, you'll know, will never die.
Whenever you want to think of me,
Remember my words so you can see

That I am always here with you
In bad times and the good times too!
There will be times when you'll feel lost
And saddened by untimely fate.
Just pray, and I'll be praying too
That your grief will never turn to hate.
My memory will be safe with you
Because I know you care for me,
And through your loving thoughts and deeds,
You will become my legacy.
Thus, I wish you safe, and I wish you well.
I'll miss you always, again I tell,
And so before I bid goodbye,
My love, you'll know, will never die.

Over the years, I've dealt with many losses in my extended family. Each time family and friends get together, we reminisce about the things we have done with those lost family members. It got me thinking about how one's life affects another and another and another. This ripple effect of love that washes over our souls during our lives never ends. I have also discovered that no single person completely knows everything about another person, no matter how close or intimate they are. We react to people in different ways and times, and throughout our entire lives, we go through different stages of growth. It is amazing how we can make many different ripples of love in one lifetime. It is also interesting that the seeds we plant grow and grow and grow even after we're gone. This is a beautiful discovery to me. I saw tangible evidence of everlasting life. If a person's life just stopped, so would the sum of their life. I feel the presence of those who've come and gone every time I see a product of their living. I heard a song by Randy Travis called "Three Wooden Crosses," and the lyrics have some examples of what I speak of.

The song talks about legacies—the things we leave behind. In the song, there is a farmer that leaves his land, his harvest, and a love for farming with his son. There is a teacher that left her wisdom with her students. There is a preacher who left faith with his dying breath, which then led to a man's vocation into priesthood.

This got me thinking about my mother and what she left behind as her legacy. In me, she left a love for life, a deep and humble faith, the love for beauty and nature, and compassion for those in need. I look at my siblings, and I see a part of her in every one of them. My mom loved making our yard beautiful. She was a very hard worker and never seemed to slow down. She always planted fruit trees, vegetables, plants, and flowers. The yard was always a wonderful place to sit and relax. It always brought a sense of abundance and joy. My brothers Dave and Benjamin have her creativity and green thumb. They love growing vegetables, planting trees, and making their spaces beautiful and thriving. My brother John Paul always goes out of his way to help anyone in need, even if he doesn't have what is needed he finds a way to help. He inherited her resourcefulness. My mother was also very competitive. That passed down to my brother Frank and most of my nieces and nephews. She loved her children without end, and she would never turn us away when we really needed help. My sisters Julie and June inherited that trait because their children are the center of their lives. My sister Helen has so many talents, but the one that stands out from my mother is her courage and her nurturing of the wounded. All of us were conditioned by my mom to respect the earth and what God has given us. We all have my mom's sense of adventure. We might have different ideas about what an adventure is, but we all venture out to discover new things. We all have a deeper faith in God because of our mother's example of unconditional love. She encouraged each of us to be individuals and to use our gifts and talents for the benefit of others. I never saw a selfish act from my mom in my entire life.

Her passing was the hardest I've ever had to deal with, but I know she is always watching over me. I feel her presence just as I know that God is always by my side. If my understanding and faith was different when my mom left this world, I would not have been able to prosper. She was my constant and the person I turned to for advice. She was home for me.

The last five years of her life were physically and emotionally difficult for her. She suffered immensely from dialysis. She could no longer walk or care for herself. Before then, she was strong as an ox. She could outlast any of her children working in the yard. In the end, her weakness played havoc with her pride. She did not want to be a burden to her children. But none of us thought she was a burden. We loved tending to her. We realized that our hardship in dealing with our emotions was nothing compared with all the years she had spent in raising eight children, each very different from the other. She and her love live on in the hearts of her children, grandchildren, and great-grandchildren.

I'm happy thinking I've learned something from those who've crossed my path and that God brought them my way as a blessing. It is also comforting to know that there is a purpose for everyone, and life is a venue of endless learning and teaching opportunities. I believe I am valuable not just to God but to the human race. Each of us makes a difference in life, with one person at a time.

Our Dearly Departed

The moments we shared were special,
Each a treasure preserved in our hearts.
The music of your laughter
Was always a beautiful art.
We will remember the fun we all had
When you'd joke or tell us some story.
We will miss you now that you have gone
To live in God's heavenly glory.
Your memory will live on forever.
We will speak your name with respect.
We will carry our cross with endurance
To lead the kind of life you'd expect.
Our adventures may not be as great,
Our gatherings may not be as much fun,
But you will always and forever be with us,
Our dearly departed, loved one.

Dry Your Teary Eye

The time has come for parting, but do not say *goodbye*;
Instead, until we meet again, dry your teary eye.
I've left some bits and pieces of myself for you to find;
You'll see in all our memories my treasures left behind.
My journey home is beautiful. I can't describe its glow;
My soul and spirit overwhelmed with love the Father shows.
His angels came to greet me and wrapped me in their wings,
While you pray for me on earth, a heavenly choir sings.
So when it is your time to come, with St. Peter, I'll patiently wait
To reunite with joyful cheers at heaven's golden gate.

Through all my grief for friends, family, and acquaintances, I've also learned that for each person I've lost, the process of grieving was very different. I found that I'd pray for the one that needed the most help. This might sound a little self-righteous, but I realized that most of my prayers were for me anyway. Each of these people had a different impact on me, and when faced with their death, I would see a reflection of how I had treated or mistreated them during their time here. Indirectly, God was teaching me how to be accountable for my actions and inactions. Because of my faith, I believe that death is an existence away from God. This would be an existence without love; therefore, I really don't believe that death exists since I know that God loves us. I believe we are transformed, we transition, we transpire into another realm of being. Our bodies die, but our souls live. These are my thoughts, and they have helped me through my grief. Consequently, I still feel their energy in my life.

A very dear friend of mine invited me to a "Soul Ascension" ceremony for her cat, Ivan. I knew how important a companion Ivan was to her, so my husband and I went in full support of her. A few of her close friends and a minister gathered in a beautiful area in a grotto to say goodbye to Ivan. The minister said an opening prayer and blessing, my friend gave a eulogy, then each of us took turns speaking about this wonderful cat that had kept her company for a few years of her life. We could describe Ivan with childlike descriptions and characterize him with virtues like patience, friendliness, energy, and so on. My husband described, in awe, Ivan's unparalleled hunting instinct as he narrated his observation of the cat's prowess and stealth. I could see how much Ivan was respected even though he was just an animal. This being, that God made, had the capacity to love and be loved. This cat, being just as he was meant to be, inspired love and admiration from the human race. I learned something that day: we should be just as God made us. It also made me think about humanity. If only we, humans, could recognize, respect, and inspire the goodness that God creates in each other. Our tendencies run to judgment of one's faults. Can you imagine a world of people who inspire and protect what God has created in each individual? I think that world would be a much safer and loving place.

Later, I asked my friend about the ceremony, and she explained that the soul ascends to a higher consciousness. I looked "soul ascension" up on the Internet, and it was defined as the process of elevating your energy and awareness into new worlds of perception, experience, and creation. There is much more to it than this, but God can do anything. This brought to mind the *ascension* of Jesus and the *assumption* of Mary into heaven. I know that heaven is a new world of perception, experience, and creation. Life after this life, we will never die. Another thing that struck me during this ceremony is that all the people there were gathered in love to support a friend suffering from the loss of a constant and loving companion.

> I said goodbye to a friend today
> In hopes that his soul will find its way
> Not to an end
> But to ascend,
> Up to the light of a new dawning day.

Prayers have always helped me to find the answers to my questions. God knows me! God knows what I am feeling. He knows when I'm sad, angry, scared, and confused. Our honest prayers reflect our true desires, and God is aware of them. When we lose someone dear to us, we can't understand why this person is no longer in our lives.

Sometimes the grief overwhelms us, and our vision is lost in the darkness of our pain. Only through prayer have I been able to understand and see clearly that life does not end when our bodies die. Hope lets me know that when our loved ones die, there is a passing of sorts—thus, a passing away. They leave us for a different realm. They move on to an everlasting life to do divine tasks. We will surely miss their presence, but their spirits and souls belong to God. I had a difficult time when people would tell me to have faith in His promises. I didn't really know what Jesus promised. I didn't really know much about faith, so I studied the Bible and the *Catechism of the Catholic Church* and found that Jesus promised that He would prepare a place for us in His Father's house (paradise or heaven) and that we would be with Him in eternity.

God grants us the hope of everlasting life. His promise is a beautiful gift, and prayer helps us to look past the sorrow of the moment to see the glory of our faith. Death is a part of life, just as night must follow day. It is a separation of our body and soul. It is the separation of the physical and the spiritual realms. We must have faith in order to heal. Since I didn't really know much about my faith or religion, I turned to the Bible. It turned out to be an excellent tool for me to learn from. Pope Benedict XVI said, "Every time we read the Bible we enter into conversation with God." So I started my conversations with God and started seeing things from a very different perspective.

The Bible is full of trials just like ours and gives us words of inspiration. As a Catholic, I believe in the *communion of saints*. This is the connection of all of us, God's children, with Jesus Christ at the head, bound by His love. It is love, and it communicates the good of each of us to one another. This connection goes beyond our earthly life, all of us—all the Saints, all the dearly departed souls, and us here on earth—as part of one body, a family in Christ that lasts forever. This spiritual union goes beyond and continues in the next life, not broken by death but destined to find fulfillment in eternal life, thanks to Jesus Christ, our risen Lord. I also had many questions about *purgatory*. Growing up, I was always a little scared when people talked about purgatory. Curiosity pushed me to research this in depth, and it is a beautiful belief, because it shows us just how much God wants us with Him.

In the glory of heaven the blessed continue joyfully to fulfill God's will in relation to other men and to all creation. Already they reign with Christ; with him they shall reign for ever and ever. Purgatory is the final purification. All who die in God's grace and friendship, but still imperfectly purified, are indeed assured of their eternal salvation; but after death they undergo purification, so as to achieve the holiness necessary to enter the joy of heaven. (CCC 1029–1030)

I see purgatory as the mud room of heaven now, a place to strip off the dirt and clean ourselves off before entering this holy place. It prepares us to meet the One who loves us the most. This is a place where we decontaminate our souls, removing all the bad bacteria that keeps us from being able to accept God's full love and presence. God thought of everything, and I know that my understanding of anything is really minuscule to what truly is. I had to put purgatory into a concept that made sense to me, and it gave me a wonderful sense of *hope*. The Bible helps us to see beyond the things we understand.

The following are some prayers for those who grieve and a few Bible verses that comfort me in times of mourning. I hope that, in the same way, they might bring you closer to a heart not so broken.

The Lord is near to the brokenhearted, and saves the crushed in spirit. (Psalms 34:18)

There are many prayers in the book of Psalms. They might help those who have never prayed before or don't really know where to start. These are common prayers, but the best prayers are those from your heart. Just speak, and the Divine hears.

Have no anxiety about anything, but in everything by prayer and supplication with thanksgiving let your requests be made known

> to God. And the peace of God, which passes all
> understanding, will keep your hearts and your
> minds in Christ Jesus. (Philippians 4:6–7)

The prayers will end in *amen*; then, a different prayer begins. This first one comes from my heart:

Lord, I know you are listening. Thank you for the time you have granted me to spend with my loved one. Please take him or her into your care. Bless him or her with eternal life, and grant him or her peace. I trust you, Lord, and I trust in your will. Please help me to see with clarity the light of your promise and take away the sorrow in my heart that pains me so deeply. Please help me through my grief and help me to let go. I cherish the time I had with my dearly departed, and thank you for all the wonderful memories you've given us together. Lord, grant me the courage to face each day without his or her physical presence, grant me comfort in my sadness, grant me faith through my doubt, and grant me hope through my despair. Lift my spirit, oh Father in heaven, because I am weak right now, and I need you. I love you, Lord, and although I don't understand your plan, please help me to find peace. Amen.

> Give ear, O Lord, to my prayer; listen to my
> cry of supplication. In the day of my trouble I call
> on you, for you do answer me. (Psalms 86:6–7)

Eternal, Holy God, I come to You burdened with worries, fears, doubts, and troubles. Calm and quiet me with peace of mind. Empty me of the anxiety that disturbs me, of the concerns that weary my spirit and weigh heavy on my heart.

Loosen my grip on the disappointments and grievances I hold on to so tightly. Release me from the pain of past hurts, of present anger and tension, of future fears.

Sometimes it's too much for me, Lord, too many demands and problems, too much sadness, suffering, and stress.

Renew me spiritually and emotionally. Give me new strength, hope, and confidence. Prepare me to meet the constant struggles of daily life with a deeper faith and trust in You.

Let your love set me free, for peace, for joy, for grace, for life, for others, forever. Amen.

Father God, your power brings us to birth, your providence guides our lives, and by Your command we return to dust. Lord, those who die still live in Your presence, their lives change but do not end. I pray in hope for my family, relatives, and friends, and for all the dead known to You alone. In company with Jesus Christ, who died and now lives, may they rejoice in Your kingdom, where all our tears are wiped away. Unite us together again in one family to sing Your praise forever and ever. Amen.

Come to me, all who labor and are heavy laden, and I will give you rest. Take my yoke upon you, and learn from me; for I am gentle and lowly in heart, and you will find rest for your souls. For my yoke is easy, and my burden is light. (Matthew 11: 28–30)

Dearest Jesus, who wept at the death of your friend and taught that they who mourn shall be comforted, grant us the comfort of your presence in our loss. Send Your Holy Spirit to direct us lest we make hasty or foolish decisions. Send Your Spirit to give us courage lest through fear we recoil from living. Send Your Spirit to bring us your peace lest bitterness, false guilt, or regret take root in our hearts.

The Lord has given. The Lord has taken away. Blessed be the name of the Lord. Amen.

O sweet mother Mary, who knew the sadness of mourning those your heart loved most, Jesus, your Son, and Joseph, your devoted spouse, pray for us in our time of loss. Amen.

In St. Teresa of Calcutta's "Varanasi Letter," she writes,

How can we last even one day living our life without hearing Jesus say, "I love you." It is impossible. Our soul needs that as much as the body needs to breathe the air. If not, prayer is

42

dead, and meditation is only thinking. Jesus wants each of us to hear Him speaking in the silence of our hearts.

When I read her letter, my heart and my mind opened even more to the presence of God, and with that *divine grace*, my eyes opened wide to the belief of life after death and the promise of Jesus Christ, which is eternal life. I've learned over the years to trust God more, and trust is essential. Through adoration and prayer, I meet Jesus every time, and I know He lives eternally.

Prayer is not asking. Prayer is putting oneself in the hands of God, at His disposition, and listening to His voice in the depth of our hearts. (St. Teresa of Calcutta)

Part 2

The Sun Sets

Darkness

The darkness came upon me in a sudden scary plight.
I wandered, stumbling blindly in the harshness of my night.
I didn't see the sun set. Its darkening was quick.
I could not find the moonlight. The cloud's gloom was too thick.
The thunder roared loudly. The storm inside me brewed,
And in my soul's deep pondering, God's light could not intrude.
My choice was not to see Him, to shut the Son's light out,
To wallow in my sadness, to grieve and mourn and pout.
How could I miss the sun set with its beauty shining bright,
Slowly fading into twilight, then gently into night.
I know God's plan is lovely. There's beauty in all things.
When faith is planted deeply, our peace can take on wings.
For with the setting sun, dark follows as does rest,
And God can bring us peace, for only God knows best.

John Donne wrote, "No man is an island." No individual can live life completely alone. We need companionship. Many of us seek a companion that completes us, a soul mate, a twin flame, someone to fill our days and nights with love and devotion. Companionship comes in so many forms, and each form is important in the shape of our lives. No single individual can meet all the needs of any other individual. Only God can. Our souls long for Him just as He longs for our souls, but in order to fulfill the needs of the soul, we must love one another. Each person has been given divine gifts in order to love, and these gifts must be used.

My life is filled with relationships. Each relationship is a trinity of sorts: between me and the other individual and with God. The Hindu word "Namaste" means "I bow to the divine in you" and in another translation means "the sacred in me recognizes the sacred in you." It explains how I feel, especially when I pray to see the face of God in others. I am confident that the Holy Spirit dwells in everyone I cross paths with.

I've had acquaintances that have blown through my life like a super typhoon, affecting certain aspects of my personality with strength and fierceness. And I've also had friends who are as steady and sure as night and day and who have influenced me over time. Every one of them has made a difference in my life. Some were lessons, but most have been blessings. Many relationships were interesting and good, but others were meant to be short-lived, and it was okay to let them go. God brings us together in His time for a specific purpose, and when that is accomplished, letting go is necessary.

I've been blessed with a wonderful husband, my soul mate. We decided to make a lifetime commitment, and then the journey of marriage began. The time I spend with him seems to slip by in an instant. Yesterday became a year, and I know the years will turn into decades. The life we are building with each other is already filled with memories of special moments and trials. It's an exciting adventure! I know that the time with a partner can change in an instant, but love that is respectfully exchanged will surpass even the boundaries of life and death. I know he will still love me after I die, and I will surely still love and cherish him if he passes first.

This is true of all intimate partnerships. We imprint a part of our makeup onto another person's life, and that impact will not fade away, so I try to make a good impact always. My marriage is fortified in the strength of the love we give each other, because we've practiced the virtues of gentleness, joy, forgiveness, patience, compassion, kindness, respect, faith, and trust.

Bill and I met in 1988. I lived with my family in Guam, and we were visiting my aunt in Washington State after I graduated from high school. I was talking with my cousins and siblings at my aunt's kitchen table when I felt strong hands on my shoulders and heard an unfamiliar voice say, "Hey, how's it goin'?" I glanced up at the person touching me and freaked out! He reminded me of a big lumberjack. I froze, my shoulders stiffened, my jaw dropped, and my eyes bugged out, because my cousins and my brother started laughing. Bill, confused, asked what was so funny. My cousin said, "Dude, she's not Carmen!" Bill looked down and noticed that I wasn't who he thought I was. He released my shoulders. He was one of my cousin's best friends and very close to my aunt's family. That was my first encounter with him. I avoided him every time he came to their house after that.

My family and I went back to Guam a few weeks later. My cousins, over the years, would mention him whenever I came to visit, but I never saw him again. When Facebook came out, we reconnected. Over the years, we'd chat and talk on the phone for short periods. I was unhappily married at that time, and Bill would talk me through some of my problems, playing advocate to my then husband, and helped me through some difficult times. He became a very dear friend. My civil marriage of thirteen years didn't last, and after my divorce, I focused on service.

My service to God called me to something bigger. I needed to establish my vocation. I wanted to volunteer as a layperson with the Missionaries of Charity. I prayed for my vocation for two years and devoted myself to service in and out of church. I would often talk to Bill during that time, but we never thought of each other in a romantic sense. He thought it was impractical because of how far we lived from each other, and I just thought of him as a buddy that I could confide in. I spoke to him about the prospect of going on mission, and he was very supportive. He even mentioned that I might meet a nice Catholic man that had the same interests. He proclaimed to be a confirmed bachelor.

One night, after mass, I lit two candles at the altar for my vocation. I asked God that if my vocation was to go on a mission, He would make the way, and if my vocation was to be a wife, to lead me to my soul mate and to keep him safe. It was a very simple prayer, and God heard me. The next day, I called Bill to see how he was doing. We talked and talked and talked for thirteen hours straight! Our relationship turned into a romance, and we've never stopped talking since. God made the way. I trusted the Lord completely, and he led me back to Washington. I left everything I was familiar with, and when I saw Bill at the airport, I felt that I'd come home. I know God's hand was in this relationship, because Bill and I hadn't physically made contact until we saw each other at the airport. But the connection we built across the miles was very intimate and fulfilling. I got to know him better through our conversations than through our physical meeting, because we made a spiritual connection uninterrupted by worldly distractions.

God works really fast! One month after our initial thirteen-hour conversation, we decided to get married; three months later, I moved to Washington. Then, three weeks later, we were married at St. Michael's Catholic Church among my family members, cousins, and some of Bill's friends. One week after that, we were married at Center for Spiritual Living, Seattle, surrounded by more of our friends and family. It was very important for us to be married in our respective churches.

When I think about it now, it was a beautiful testament of faith bringing people together, instead of religions separating because of customs. We respected each other's path to God, and it, in turn, made me more faithful. Marriage in Catholicism is a sacrament of service. The sacraments were given to us by Jesus Christ to consummate our worldly lives to a life in God's grace. As a spouse, we serve each other in love and cooperation. The fruit of the spirit become fine-tuned, and in this practice of unconditional love, the vocation of marriage benefits society as a whole. It becomes a testimony of love and fellowship.

> But the fruit of the Spirit is love, joy, peace, patience, kindness, goodness, faithfulness, gentleness, self-control; against such there is no law. (Galatians 5: 22–23)

Marriage is a reflection of the relationship between God and the church, so I wanted to let Bill know how I felt about marriage before he committed himself to me. Before I left Guam, I wrote him this letter:

> My Beloved Billy,
>
> I look forward to begin this new chapter in our lives. We embark on this journey into a covenant with each other and with God together. I am confident that the beauty of our love will grow, will spread, and will be fruitful, for all good things grow with God. As we enter into this sacrament of Holy Matrimony we become soul mates, mated for life and responsible for one another until we pass away. I am honored God chose me for you, because you are a wonderful man with a beautiful and kindred soul. I couldn't have asked for someone more suited and perfect for me. You build me up and make me feel worthy of my calling.
>
> In the Bible we are constantly told to live in the Spirit. To choose the spirit over the flesh. Marriage is unlike all other sacraments in that it requires us to live as one in the flesh and grow together in the spirit. All other sacraments are intended for the individual relationship with God. Marriage unites us to each other and us to God.
>
> There is something that many non-Catholics or reformed-Catholics don't understand and

it's called sacrificial love. It is thought that we shouldn't have to sacrifice anything for another person's love, that love is based on the conditions of what is sacrificed, but this concept is misconstrued and misunderstood. Sacrificial love is meant for the one giving, not for the one receiving. It means that you are loved more than any THING of this world. That you are more important than something I'd like, like to do or want to get. That you come first and that your needs matter. It is unselfish and desiring to give completely of oneself. It means that I will love you even if I am not loved back, completely unconditional. Catholics believe this because it was the last act of Jesus Christ. He laid His life down because He loved enough to sacrifice His flesh for us and we are called to do the same, to love without terms.

I will promise to love you with that kind of sacrificial love, because you matter, Billy! You are important and you will be a part of me. Thank you for agreeing to marry me in the Catholic Church. I know your reasons are not sacramental, but I wanted you to understand why it is so important to me. God bless you, my beloved, and have a wonderful day.

Yours Truly,
Ruthie

We've had a wonderful adventure so far, and I'm sure our journey will last for a long time. When life ends, we'll still have these adventures etched in our souls. I am confident that love will carry us into the next chapter.

No one's life is perfect, and no relationship is without its ups and downs, but when you are committed to a person wholeheartedly, a lifetime is not long enough. Many trials in life can bring distress, but treating each other with patience, respect, decency, and commitment are paramount to succeed in overcoming the obstacles of any relationship. This is the struggle of love. As a Catholic, we have many, many traditions that call for complete devotion, such as attending mass every Sunday. Many times, these devotionals feel like work and obligation instead of contemplative or meditative prayer, but whenever I have committed to putting faith first, these traditions have turned out to bring me such joy, peace, strength, and courage. These are my tasks of love. It takes work, and it takes divine grace to last. Like my physical devotion to God, I will try to replicate that in my relationship with my spouse. It is through the tragedies and trials of life that test our charity. You find support and commitment in love, and that strength in unconditional love is what makes a relationship last. It takes faith, hope, and love.

> Love is patient and kind; love is not jealous or boastful; it is not arrogant or rude. Love does not insist on its own way; it is not irritable or resentful; it does not rejoice at wrong, but rejoices in the right. Love bears all things, believes all things, hopes all things, endures all things. (1 Corinthians 13:4–7)

Lifelong partnerships are not easy to part with. So too the following poems were not easy to write. The death of someone who has shared your deepest affection is traumatic. How should we deal with that tragedy? I could only imagine how I would handle the loss of my husband, who is now my best friend. Therefore, in faith, hope, and love, but most especially love, I wrote these words for those who have lost their companions suddenly. After the day, the sun sets. I hope these poems portray the meaning of everlasting love and that these impressions will help you through the night so that maybe you can see a beautiful sun rise.

For as we share abundantly in Christ's sufferings, so through Christ we share abundantly in comfort too. (2 Corinthians 1:5)

The Vows

I vowed to love and cherish you.
I vowed to be your friend.
I vowed that through our lifetimes
My love would never end.
I vowed to be there for you.
I promised to be kind.
I made myself available
To comfort your heart and mind.
I vowed to show forgiveness
And to share my life with you.
To be a life companion
In faithfulness and truth.
My heart now is conflicted
Because you left me here.
I thought I'd live forever
With the safety of you near.
I never did consider
That one of us would leave,
But I pray you rest in peace, my dear,
As I mend our broken weave.

How Can I Forget You?

How can I forget you when your love is oh so strong?
It surpassed every boundary you have crossed.
Your love withstood the test of time and conquered all the odds.
Now in my loneliness for you, I'm lost.
In sudden death, your light went out but still shines on my soul,
Reflecting every teardrop from my eye.
There's a pain that lingers in my chest, like a piercing from a knife,

Because I had no chance to say goodbye.
Our memories flood every thought and come pouring down like rain.
Death shadows all the joy my heart could feel.
For having even spent a day in your awesome love,
My days without you now seem so unreal.
So I will never forget you, because your love was, oh, so strong!
But my life will never ever be the same.
Your death has left me empty and longing for your embrace.
But your love will carry me through all the pain.

How Do I?

How can I think of tomorrow when my love left me today?
He said he'd always be here, but God took him away.
I wish the sun would not come up; I want to stay in bed.
I cannot really face the fact that he is really dead.
He went away so suddenly...we couldn't say goodbye
And now my only solace is to stay in bed and cry.
How do I start my life again? I haven't got a clue.
The thought of going on without him leaves me hopelessly blue.
How do I get up and go on when my life revolved around him?
Every vision of my future is dark and gray and dim.
How do I get through yet another day without his tender touch?
How do I go on when I miss him so much?

To Grace

An angel sat beside me once and sang a song to me.
She knew my soul was tired, and she felt I needed rest.
Reverently, I listened but could not understand the words,
But the music of it filled my heart, and I knew God loved me so.
I know her song was a prayer, because I felt my heart restored.
My sorrow dissipated, my mind refreshed, renewed,
And my guardian had wrapped me like a child in her wings,
Protecting me from worldly woes and guided me to grace.

It is truly a blessing when God brings two people together to share a life. I urge you to show your affection to the ones you hold dear to your hearts while you can, because we never know when things will change. The song "If Tomorrow Never Comes" by George Straight sums up nicely that we need to let those we love know how we feel before it is too late.

> I have found the paradox, that if you love until it hurts, there can be no more hurt, only more love. (St. Teresa of Calcutta)

That Moment

I received a call from the morgue that brought me to
    my knees.
In that moment
the clear glass window that made the world look so
    beautiful shattered to the ground, no longer pro-
    tecting me from the wind, the rain, the cold.
In that moment
the wood that made the wall that made me feel safe
    and secure shook and came crumbling down.
In that moment
the sun that gave me light and kept me warm each
    day hid behind clouds that thundered and roared
    brewing up a storm that chilled me to my very
    bones.
In that moment
the path that led me to the hope of a prosperous future
    became a gorge impossible to cross.
In that moment
faith was forgotten.
Then I received a call from God that brought me to
    my knees, and He said,
"My child, in this moment, turn your head up and
    remember me. Let me have your heart to keep in

heaven, and I will heal you. My Son, who gave His life, is the glass that amplifies beauty and protects you from the world. Life in Him is shatterproof. My cross is the wood that has saved you and will always protect you. My Son will calm the storm in one breath. He is the light of the world, the light unto your path. I have always been with you. Have faith."

Heaven Sent

Love fills your heart when you give it away,
For love does not grow if you keep it at bay.
Your heart does not empty; instead, it will fill,
Because showing love is truly God's will.
You filled me up, and my heart overflowed
With kindness and care, so my spirit glowed.
Your love made me want to continue to share
To give and support, to trust and to care.
You're gentle and kind and remained by my side,
A friend to hold on to. In you, I'd confide.
My spirit was blessed with your love and your grace
I hope it's reflected when you think of my face.
Each breath I took with you was a wish coming true
Whenever you're near, hopes and dreams are renewed
Your love's unconditional, and my life is content.
You're the love of my life and heavenly sent.

Love Will Heal

In the light of each new day,
I hope His grace will shine your way.
Your faith in God will make you whole,
And LOVE will heal your grieving soul.
Don't cry for me too long, for I'm with you.
Each time you reminisce, my soul rejoices too.

I'm safely in our Father's care; you seem so far away,
But think of me with loving thoughts,
and with your heart, please pray.
I'll wait for you at heaven's gate and greet you when you come,
For God's great plan is to bring you here
when your tasks on earth are done.

Clarity

Sadness filled my soul today.
The grief would not subside.
Sorrow overwhelmed my heart.
It would not cease. I cried.
Your death has left me helpless.
I refuse to face the day.
The hopes and dreams we shared before
Have dimmed and gone away.
Our friends and family have come around
To try to help me through,
But when they've gone back to their lives,
I'll only think of you.
My thoughts just cloud reality.
I really need to pray
For God to give me clarity
And peace to find my way.

Brooding

A chapter in our lives is over, but I'll hold you close to me.
You brought such joy and laughter. Now, my disability.
Without your spirit near me, without you clear in sight.
My happiness was around you; my loss is now my plight.
You were a precious jewel in the midst of all the rubble.
Your life inspired me all around, your death just burst my bubble.
I do not want to turn the page. I know it won't be good.

Why did your passing incite such rage?
When will time change my mood?

Drama—life is full of drama. There are some tragedies in life we must go through alone, and some we need others to help us get through. Each of these situations leaves a memory and an emotional tie. Mostly, we remember the fear, the suffering, the doubt, and especially, the hurt. We don't realize the impact our faith has on how we deal with the situation and whether or not we can pull through. When we survive these times, our faith, our hope, and our love usually increase, because when we don't know what to do or have no control over the outcome of something, we turn to faith, and we want to hope. Faith and hope can humble and help us to release our pain. We try to remain confident that things will work out, or we pray for divine intervention to change the circumstances. We hope that what is troubling us will ease. These are the times when family and friends should come together to make love visible. The death of a companion is one of these times.

When we love someone and promise to share our life with them, we risk the chance of rejection and heartache: rejection during the time we are together and heartache when we part. When the sun sets and our loved one is called to their eternal life, it is the most difficult form of heartache because it seems permanent. But are we really apart? I believe, wholeheartedly, that in our memories, we carry our loved ones with us forever. Love binds us together in both life and death. A partnership makes us strong in many ways, but weak in others. We have to understand that if we really love unconditionally while we are alive, we can get through any hardship, even the heartache of parting. The communion of saints surpasses even the boundary of death. It connects our spirits in one body of Christ, one community of beings connected through love in whatever realm we are in—physical or spiritual. That is why we pray for our dearly departed and why we ask our friends, as well as the saints, the angels, and the Blessed Mother to intercede for us.

Love is unfailing, and in its infinite kindness, trust, respect, forgiveness, humility, and understanding, it has the capability to turn the bitterness of life into a positive force. The tragedies of our lives add to love's fullness, for without sorrow, we would never recognize our blessings. Therefore, we must rejoice that life with our partner was a blessing and that the hard times contributed to the strength of the love we exchanged. We should carry that contentment in our hearts.

Without these dramatic life situations, we probably would never know what goodness is or appreciate the people whom we turn to for help. At the loss of a spouse, who played the most intimate role in our life, we feel lost. We have to get used to our individuality and the fact that they are no longer with us, to help, console, or live with us. During your time of loss, I pray that you will have the strength to say goodbye and the fortitude of faith to believe that they live beyond us now.

> But they who wait for the Lord shall renew
> their strength, they shall mount up with wings
> like eagles, they shall run and not be weary, they
> shall walk and not faint. (Isaiah 40:31)

Lord, you are attentive to the voice of our pleading. Let us find, in your Son, comfort in our sadness, certainty in our doubt, and courage to live through this hour. Make our faith strong through Christ our Lord. Amen

Lord, my loved one is gone now from this earthly dwelling and has left behind those who mourn their absence. Grant that we may hold their memory dear, never bitter from what we have lost nor in regret for the past but always in hope of the eternal kingdom where you will bring us together again. We ask this through Christ our Lord. Amen.

What Happened?

You said, "Good morning," with a smile
when you first saw me today.
You kissed me goodbye before you went on your way.
You called to ask, "Hi, and how are you doing?"
You said something kind when my frustration was brewing.
You forgave when we fought and let slight mishaps go.

You cared for what I thought and always made sure I'd know.
You gave gestures of love from beginning to end,
Always made me happy with my heart wide open.
But now that you've gone to join God and His angels,
My mind is detached and my thoughts are all mangled.
You passed in the night, which took me by surprise.
How can I see the light through the tears in my eyes?
Darkness surrounds me, and the gloom's all around.
It feels like my life has been bitten by hell's hound.
Your love was so beautiful, and now that you're gone,
I want to give up; I don't want to go on.

Captive

My spirit is held captive as you weep in sorrow's throng.
The power of your emptiness is really holding strong.
It keeps me from the Father 'cause it shadows all the light.
My soul just keeps on searching, and you need to end my plight.
I know you miss me dearly. I truly miss you too,
But I want some peace and quiet that are now long overdue.
Lift your sadness to our Savior; He'll ease the pain you feel.
He'll give you strength and guidance to cope with what is real.
I'll love you always, sweetheart, but your life is yours to live.
It isn't here to waste away with flowing tears of grief.
The Lord will never give you anything you cannot bear.
He will carry you to high ground if you ask in humble prayer.
So let me go in peace, my dear, and pray for me with love.
Peace be with you always, and I'll pray for you above.

> And I tell you, Ask, and it will be given
> you; seek, and you will find; knock, and it will be
> opened to you. For every one who asks receives;
> and he who seeks finds, and to him who knocks
> it will be opened. (Luke 11:9–10)

Love Lives On

You may think my passing has severed all our ties,
But listen closely to the whispers in the air.
For love will conquer boundaries and withstand the test of time.
You'll hear my voice say softly, "I am near."
Love is patient, kind, and true and holds no grudge too long.
Forgiveness can defeat the sting of lies.
Words cannot define the power of love's reign.
It grows with truth and never really dies.
Death can never hold us down nor kill the love we shared.
Love changes form and shape but still remains.
This gift God gives us each to find will overcome all odds,
Uniting us without the bonds of chains.
I never will forget you 'cause your love is true and strong.
It surpasses all the boundaries I have crossed.
Although you cannot see me, my grace lives there with you.
Our love lives on and never will be lost.

When You Came

Life was different before you came.
The storms I went through always brought pain.
Then healing came, and away went the rain.
You united our lives and gave me your name.
I always yearned for something new,
An exciting adventure or fun thing to do.
I realized I was searching for you,
A love so deep, so real, so true.
Then my skies were blue and clear.
The sun shone bright year after year.
My eyes didn't shed as many a tear.
Your love chased away all my fear.
Now another chapter unfolds in my life.
Your sudden passing cuts like a knife.
I'm thrown into turmoil and deep despair.

I feel like my lungs cannot hold any air.
Open my eyes, Lord, and help me to see
That you hold in your hands my tranquility.
Love never is lost, but it's hiding its face.
Help me through this great loss, bless me...with your grace.

> Beloved, if God so loved us, we also ought
> to love one another. No man has ever seen God;
> if we love one another, God abides in us and his
> love is perfected in us. (1 John 4:11–12)

The Love of You

God blessed me with the love of you.
- He tuned my ears so I could hear the music of your soul.
- He enhanced my sense of touch so I could feel the embrace of your love.
- He touched my nose so I could smell the sweet aroma of your grace.
- He blessed my mouth so I could taste the fruits of your spirit.
- He focused my eyes and let me see His beauty in you.
- He opened my soul so I could be your mate.

God blessed me with the love of you.

I Loved

I loved...
...the way your touch made my body tingle from head to toe.
...the way your voice made my ears burn and my heart leap.
...the way your lips melted all my worries away.
...the way your eyes told me that I was beautiful and wanted.
...the way your smell penetrated my senses
and triggered wonderful memories.
...the way your presence surrounded me
with sanctuary and protection.

…the way your love consumed me.
I miss…
…your touch.
…your voice.
…your lips.
…your eyes.
…your smell.
…your presence.
…your love.

Nightmare

I woke up this morning, and you were not there
To touch my cheek, to kiss my lips,
To stroke my hair.
Were you in a hurry and have to run?
Did you even come home?
Were you out having fun?
I had a bad nightmare. You died in a crash!
I couldn't breathe. My world turned dark,
My dreams to ash.
The earth moved beneath me, and Satan got hold.
I was mad. I was scared.
I was devilishly cold.
When I woke up today, it gave me a start.
When I reached to my side, you were gone…
With my heart.
Was my bad nightmare true? Yes, it happened that way!
It's coming back. I remember now:
Live day by day.

My Love Surrounds You

Although I am not in the world of the living, I am alive.
You may not be able to see me, but I am right in front of you.

You may not think you can feel me, but I am
the breeze that caresses your skin.
Love has no bounds, so even if my soul has
passed into the realm of spirits,
I surround you with my love.
There is a glow inside my spirit that explodes
every time you think of me.
The magic of your love surrounds me and wraps around my being.
Even if we are physically apart, you still
and always will bring me joy.
I am smiling!

Before I Wake

Kiss me softly in the morning light before I start the day.
Hug me tightly and hold me close, and never go away.
When I awake, you won't be near, but I will be okay.
Because your kiss upon my lips will last throughout the day.
Caress me gently before I wake, and whisper sweet words in my ear.
Just hold my hand and pray with me to ward away my tears.
For in my dreams, you live with me to love me and to care.
When I awake, my mind will be full of the beautiful voice I still hear.
Talk to me within my dreams before the dawn's first light,
For once I open my eyes to it, you disappear from sight.
I know that it's time to let you go, and I know I'll be all right,
But with you still near before I wake, I have the will to fight.

A friend of mine just recently lost her husband of forty-three years. She was sharing with me her husband's suffering and struggle with cancer and that now he rests. She's a very faithful woman and truly believes in the promises of Christ. We were praying together, and she was so thankful to God for the distraction He graced her with. Her husband had passed away, but her son had just had twins. She was saying, "Thank you, Lord, for letting me see the blessings, even when my heart was hurting, because now I've found peace with my husband's passing. Take care of him, please, and thank you for ending his pain." Her prayer taught me a lot about trust. How a person's trust in the Lord can heal our brokenness. I pray that the Lord comforts you through this time and brings you to a point where you can feel joy again.

Separation

We enjoyed so many ventures in life
And were doubtful of many a thing,
But as we found that time is obscure,
Our hope in the present would spring.
Together we made the best of our time,
But little did we know
That life had yet another path,
Leaving little time to grow.
The chapters of our storybook
Would soon be at an end,
For we would walk our separate paths
And turn a different bend.
You went on to grieve for me,
And I went to heaven's gate.
You're saddened by the loss of me
But accept that it is fate.
We had a wonderful time together
During our precious mile,
But down the road, your heart will heal,
And once again, you'll smile.
My wish for you is to hope again,
And I pray you will start living,
Because life is too short to waste with tears…
Of sorrow and of grieving.

My Blessing

If death should come to me tomorrow,
Don't ever weep for me in sorrow

Through joyous tears, remember me.
Stay not in mournful misery.
Throughout my life, I've been content
With all the blessings Father sent,
And in all His blessings bestowed on me,
His love, through you, has set me free.
I have been kind throughout my life.
I'm grateful even for the strife
And though I don't understand His ways,
My faith in God leads me through the maze.
So if death comes knocking at my door,
I'll say goodbye, but grieve no more.
My life has been a blessing true
Because I have been loved by you.

Part 3

Let the Children Come

Love—there is so much we can learn about love from children. They love us no matter how impatient or unfair we can be and forgive us just because they love us. Their love is truly unconditional. The dictionary defines *love* as a strong affection, attraction, or warm attachment. But children have it right. They love without purpose, without intent, without expectation, without forethought. Their love does not waiver in anger or neglect, and they can truly forgive a wrong done to them after a simple "sorry." And when they forgive, they forget. Their forgiveness is complete, their hurt is released, and then all is well. A child's love is special and innocent. You can feel it the moment you look into their eyes or feel their sweet, gentle touch. They possess purity of heart.

> But Jesus said, "Let the children come to
> me, and do not hinder them; for to such belongs
> the kingdom of heaven. (Matthew 19:14)

I have been surrounded by children my whole life, and I've been blessed with the excitement and joy of watching them grow and develop as individuals. Their love is at the core of my heart, because this kind of love is an example of truth. It is unconditional and given freely. It is a constant reminder that God's love is never failing, and it helps me to see that life is blessed regardless of any faults and tragedies. Children make us smile and laugh and let us see the wonder of life through their innocent eyes.

How do we deal with the loss of a child? How are we supposed to accept the fact that our child has passed away before we do? The natural order is that the parent dies before the child. Therefore, it is understandable to assume that a child's passing is unnatural. We raise them so they can be productive adults, to carry on our legacy of charity, to portray the kind of care we've taught them to give. A child's death destroys the natural order of things. I can only imagine what it must feel like to lose a child, and when I decided to write this section, I had to empathize with mothers who have actually lost a child. I've talked to several people, all with different stories and different outcomes. Most of the mothers I've talked to never really came to terms with the loss of their son or daughter. My heart breaks for them, but I could not fathom this kind of hurt. I included the verse Matthew 19:14, because I felt that if a child dies, they must automatically be in the kingdom of heaven. After all, Jesus did say it.

I don't think I could ever grasp that kind of suffering, but I know the Blessed Mother could tell us a thing or two about how to come to peace with the suffering and the loss. Since I'm Catholic, the Blessed Mother is a big part of my life, so I turned to her. Mary understood that we belong to God first. She understood that everything comes from God, the Father, the Creator, according to His will. She also kept her heart in heaven, always looking up and trusting in God's will. As much as she loved her son, she found her strength in God. I was contemplating on the rosary for guidance. As we say the rosary, we walk with Mary through the life, death, and resurrection of Jesus, her son, true God and true man. The *joyful mysteries* gave me a lot of insight and empathy for mothers. When I meditated on the *sorrowful mysteries*, I felt that I should always keep my heart in heaven. Then I had an urge to watch Mel Gibson's *The Passion of the Christ*. My heart and soul broke! There is such great love in the intimacy of parenthood. I couldn't stop crying. Mary constantly gave Jesus strength in His suffering. She is such a faithful and humble servant of God yet so powerful in her love for Jesus. Mother Mary has been a source of comfort for many who suffer, so I would definitely turn to her in my grief-stricken weakness.

I know that if I had lost my child, my faith would take a hard hit. I've been surrounded by children all my life. My nieces and nephews, and some of the neighborhood kids, were a huge part of my life. If anything happened to any of them, my heart would crumble. The history we share is ingrained in the fabric of my life, and they are a part of my makeup. I would ask why. I would probably be stuck in the first stage of grief for a very long time. I know myself well enough to assume that I would be depressed and lost. My life would tumble into chaos. How can we not be angry with God for taking a child before us, or rather, away from us? Faith is knowing that Jesus's promise will be fulfilled, and that my child is in paradise with Him.

> And Jesus said to him, "If you can! All things are possible to him who believes." Immediately the father of the child cried out and said, "I believe; help my unbelief!" (Mark 9:23–24)

I'm very grateful I was raised Catholic and that our faith was infused in my culture, because our traditions have me saying the rosary and turning to the Blessed Mother for consolation. The *sorrowful mysteries* bring me through the suffering of Christ and the strength of Mary, His mother, my Blessed Mother. How strong she was and what an example of humility, trust, grace, and love. She drew her strength from the Lord, and she was there for every step of Jesus's suffering, giving Him strength through love. Then, in the *glorious mysteries*, we walk through the resurrection and the reuniting of mother and son. It is a beautiful prayer, and to contemplate on the resurrection of Jesus could be a healing balm to my wounded soul. This faith would bring me solace in the fact that my child is living in the glory of paradise, that whatever suffering my baby (no matter what age) was going through does not hurt him or her anymore, and that he or she is now in the kingdom of heaven in the arms of Jesus. Also, that if I remain faithful, my soul will reunite with my child in eternal life. How beautiful the concept! I believe that we belong to God first. I have faith in this concept wholeheartedly, and I would need it to get through such an event. He breathed life into us even before we were born. We are God's creation made in God's own likeness and image; therefore, we are perfectly made with the gifts and talents we are born with and develop. But we are on borrowed time, and each of us has a purpose in life during the time our hearts are beating. I use the term "borrowed time," because our bodies are limited to a certain amount of time, but time and space is irrelevant in Spirit. When we tap into the Holy Spirit, the universe opens us up to a bigger world, a world that can heal our sadness. It would take humility. I would need to trust God's plan and believe that my child performed their preset task and was called home. It may be that they were sent to teach me how to love with all my heart, all my mind, and all my strength. This is the way we are supposed to love each other. Consequently, in this process, this is how we show our love to God. Therefore, whether the child died of natural or unnatural causes, God has them in His care. Their life had a specific purpose that was accomplished.

> At that time the disciples came to Jesus, saying, "Who is the greatest in the kingdom of heaven?" And calling to him a child, he put him in the midst of them, and said, "Truly, I say to you, unless you turn and become like children, you will never enter the kingdom of heaven. Whoever humbles himself like this child, he is the greatest in the kingdom of heaven." (Matthew 18:1–4)

Oh, Help Me Understand

Oh, Blessed Mother, help me understand
The purpose of this misery and grief inside my soul.
Let me walk into the light and feel God's grace abide,
For I cannot forge my heart against the pain that dwells inside.
Oh, Blessed Mother, help me, please intercede for me

That God will mend my wounds and heal me emotionally.

I was still looking for something in the Bible that would maybe open my eyes to such a tragedy, and I found the story of Isaac, whom Abraham was willing to sacrifice as an offering to God. Isaac was the miracle child of Abraham. He was a gift of faith from God when Abraham and Sarah were too old to have a child in the physical sense. I could not fathom the reasoning behind this willingness to sacrifice his miracle child, so I prayed for understanding. My question was answered like this. We have been loved by God since the beginning of our existence, and God will not abandon us when we trust Him. We are more than a physical being. We are soul and spirit as well. God calls us to him and tries to teach us to live in the spirit, as well as the flesh, but there is no better place for us than in God's space. This calls for absolute trust in God's sovereignty. When our flesh is done, when our bodies give up, we live on, and our spirits return to a life with God. Our life on earth is a gift to others from God, and we are to love others while we exist in the physical world. God made us perfect, and in our souls lies the truth of our being.

I was touched by a song by Selah called "I Will Carry You [Audrey's Song]." It is about a mother who lost her infant daughter. She declares her love for the child. Though others call her brave, her feeling of weakness brings her to a state of faith that looks beyond her loss and opens her ears to the voice of God. She had had so many plans for the child. God compares their plans and tells her that he has not abandoned either of them. She succumbs to His will, knowing that God's love is unparalleled.

I recall a time in my childhood that changed my perception of love. I was nearly five years old, sitting on my mother's lap. I was hugging her and told her emphatically that I loved her more than anyone else, even God.

She chuckled and responded, "Sweetheart, you cannot love me more than God. You must love God most of all because He gave you to me, and he gave me to you."

So I said, "Okay, then I love you most after God."

I was confused, but I was extremely grateful that He had picked my mother to be my mother and my family to be my family. This memory has stayed with me my whole life. It opened my eyes to see beyond this earthly life. I began to trust in the Lord from that moment. It was the best lesson in faith I could ever learn. It is very difficult to trust in God's plans if our perception is limited to what we think we know. I have matured in my faith because I know that my perception is limited to what I think I know. But God's perception is not limited.

Only God can give us peace of mind. We have to trust in the Lord's sovereignty. We don't think the way God thinks, and we don't see the greater picture; we don't see the eternal picture.

The loss of your child is one of the toughest things to come to terms with. Losing a child may seem like losing a part of yourself. How do you cope with losing a part of yourself? Could you give yourself up to God and let the Spirit take care of you? Could you love your child enough to let him or her go with grace into God's care? Lao Tzu said, "Being deeply loved by someone gives you strength, while loving someone deeply gives you courage." I don't think there is any deeper love than that which is shared between parent and child. I hope the love you have exchanged gives you faith and hope to remain strong and courageous. My prayers are with you.

God, our Father, your power brings us to birth, your providence guides our lives, and by your command, we return to dust. Lord, those who die still live in Your presence; their lives change but do not end. I pray in hope for my son or daughter, my family, relatives, and friends, and for all the dead known to You alone. May they rejoice where all our tears are wiped away, in Your kingdom in company with Christ, who died and now lives. Unite us together again in one family, to sing Your praise forever and ever.

Lord, bless me with healing, and open my eyes to the wisdom of your plan. Bless me with a heart of acceptance and humility that I may hand my child over to you and know that he or she is in your loving hands. You are Creator of all, with unfailing love, so I ask you, wholeheartedly, to please forgive me for my anger. Help me to cope, and please give me strength. Thank you for entrusting me with his or her care while he or she was here on earth. He or she was a beautiful blessing in my life, and I will forever be grateful to you. Please take him or her into Your perfect care. I release and let go. Amen.

I hope that the poems you are about to read will help transition you to the seventh stage of grief a little quicker.

I died today, and His voice filled my soul.
It was everywhere and nowhere.
Distinguished yet vague, but I knew it was calling me home.

Help Me Believe

Oh Lord, my God, why did you take him away?
My heart is suffering day after day.
How do I get over the loss of my child?
My unanswered questions are driving me wild.
I feel I'll lose faith, for I'm struggling within,
And I'm praying my pain will not cause me to sin.
Lord, please comfort my mind and grant me reprieve.
When you summoned my child, you left me to grieve.
With the last of his breath, my fortress has tumbled.
I blamed you for my heartache because
my world had just crumbled.
I need now your guidance to bring me to peace,
To understand that my child was only on lease.
We are all your children; I know this is true,
But help me believe my beautiful child is with You.

The Plans

Within my womb, a child grew,
A precious life, a gift from You.
You entrusted this soul into my care
Until he was called to serve there.
The plans I had for this cherished one
Was to follow the path of Your loving Son.

71

I wanted to share so many things,
But I guess your plan was to give him wings.
The times we spent down here on earth
Were precious to me and beyond worldly worth.
I'm saddened so by the loss of my treasure,
But I know he wasn't sent for my pleasure.
My loving Father, please lighten my heart
And let the healing of Your love start.
I'll trust You completely, as I know I should do.
I relinquish my hold and give my child to You.

How Can This Be

She can't be gone! I'm supposed to go first!
You're lying to me! It couldn't be right!
You say that my child has gone to our Maker,
No longer is with us, passed into the night!
You say that my child lies still in the morgue,
Her eyes unable to see a new day.
This is cruel and heartbreaking; it cannot be true!
What kind of prank are you trying to play?
How could this happen? How can this be?
How could God shatter my faithful heart so?
Oh, Lord, why did you do this? Why did you take her away?
I cannot survive or manage this blow.
She grew in my womb and was born beautiful.
She was precious and kind, and all I could see,
Such a light to our world that couldn't be hidden.
Why did Our Father call her before me?
Her life was ahead of her and should have been long.
Her passing away seems instinctively wrong.
The unnatural feeling of my child not here
Is unbearably painful to process and learn.
To trade places with her in this troublesome passing,
Forever my heart will continually yearn.

My Unbelief

Sent to me as a gift from above,
God presented a daughter to me to love.
To raise with tenderness, love, and care.
To teach about life and the trials we bear.
When my duty as a parent ended,
I told the Lord I was offended.
I did not trust God's will for me
And turned my back on Him angrily.
I felt betrayed, inside turned cold,
But God reminded me of my mold.
He made me see His love for me
And granted me strength and tranquility.
He said, "My child, do not fear,
Of all your concerns, I am aware.
The child you bore is in my care
And when it's time, you'll see her here.
Have faith in the promise my Son has made,
For with His sacrifice, your debt was paid.
I will help your pain to fade
Just trust me with the plan I've laid."
I'm sorry, Lord, if I've offended thee.
Please grant me courage and serenity.
Help me have patience to conquer my beast
So with my child in heaven, we will share in Your feast.

Your Life

I was so excited when I found out you were coming.
I knew the Lord had blessed me with this gift.
When you came into my world, my heart had so much joy.
Your presence gave my life a needed lift.
Your early years were wonderful. You learned so many things.
I felt so happy in the joy you brought.
Your patience, kindness, and your love just kept compiling.

Through that patience, love, and kindness, I was taught.
Adolescence was a challenge to keep you on God's path.
You were so determined that you knew.
Prayers for guidance kept you from my wrath.
God made me see His glory shine through you.
Your teenage years were so surprising
because you became my friend.
Your outlook was so understanding with wisdom in your eye.
Then God wrote yet another chapter—your life came to an end.
My loss caused me to ask Our Father, "Why?"
A mother's loving is unique. The pain of loss is deep,
So how could God's love ever bring me peace?
Then He said to me quite loudly, "Woman, do not weep!
I gave my Son, and through Him, life will never cease."
Then He opened up my eyes and said, "Behold, your babe."
Your image portrayed the beauty of your heart.
Our love for Jesus Christ had laid a path well paved.
Now healing brings a brand-new course to chart.

With You

God sent me his child to nurture and know
For nine short months in my womb would grow.
With expectant love, it was time to be born,
But our loving God called my baby back home.
Our understanding is lost in His plans,
But we have to commend her soul in God's hands.
Lord, grant us the grace to accept our great burden,
And bless us with peace that she's with you in heaven.

Is It You

Is it you, my child, that I feel in the air?
Is it you that speaks to me in dreams?
Is it you, my sweetheart, that lifts up my hair?
Is it you that makes my eyes gloss and gleam?

Are you an angel that guards my way?
Or a star that shines at night?
Do you pray for my healing every day?
Did you become my guiding light?
My love for you built and grew
From the very start.
I know you're here, my child.
I can feel it in my heart.

Then I Remembered

I thought I heard you playing today.
It was in the afternoon.
It sounded like your laughter
Was coming from your room,
Then I remembered…

I thought I saw you dreaming.
I heard you sing a song.
I smelled your favorite pillow.
Your scent was still so strong.
Then I remembered…

I thought I felt you touch me,
A light kiss on my cheek.
I thought you were hiding from me
While we were playing hide-and-seek,
Then I remembered…

I remembered when they told me.
I remembered that you're gone.
I remembered how my heart broke.
I remembered God took you home.
I remembered…

God of hope, we come to you in shock and grief and confusion of heart. Help us to find peace in the knowledge of your loving mercy to all your children, and give us light to guide us out of our darkness into the assurance of your love, in Jesus Christ our Lord. Amen.

My cousin Therese was taken by cancer at the age of forty-two. She was sweet, beautiful, kind, and very creative. Although Therese was a mother, a wife, and a sister, an adult when she passed, she was my aunt's only daughter. Therese wasn't a baby by any means, but her mother, my aunt, has never stopped grieving for her "baby girl." Everyone still misses Therese, but my aunt has been affected more deeply. Therese's passing threw her into a very deep depression that has never completely gone away.

My Auntie Cee has always been a very strong woman. She's a mother of six sons and a daughter, a wife, and a cancer survivor. She was married at the very early age of fifteen, and her family has been her life since then. Therese was already at a late stage of cancer when my aunt found out Therese was sick. My aunt, a cancer survivor herself, hoped that her daughter would beat this disease, but she also knew the stress they were in for. Therese's cancer was very different from my aunt's: it was much more aggressive. In a very deep conversation with my aunt one day, I asked her about Therese's death. This is what she told me, "Therese became very weak toward the end. I would go over to her house and help with the household chores and with the twins. It was a very emotional time for all of us. I was folding clothes in her room when Therese said, 'Mom, I'm dying.' I put the clothes down and went to my daughter's bedside. I sat up at the edge of her bed and picked my daughter up into my lap. She was so light, but I held her in my arms. I stroke her hair as I did when she was a child and said, 'I know, sweetheart. It's okay.' Therese closed her eyes, and my daughter died in my arms."

With tears in our eyes, I hugged Auntie Cee and felt the sorrow she still held in her heart. So much pain, and what I felt must have been only a sliver of what she felt. The whole family was devastated, and almost immediately after, my uncle Joe's health deteriorated. He suffered through dementia, and my aunt took care of him. She had to be strong because dementia is very emotionally difficult for a family. His disease kept my aunt so busy that I don't think she was ever really able to grieve for Therese. After four years, her husband passed away. My aunt grieved for them both, and her life completely changed. Despite her sons' efforts to comfort her, she felt alone, and she felt lost. The four years she spent taking care of Uncle Joe gave her purpose and kept her busy. Without purpose, she fell into a deeper depression.

Therese was her only daughter, and they shared a special bond that only mothers and daughters do. Whenever my aunt and I spend time together, she tells me about things they had done together. We've gone to places Therese used to take her, and my aunt would reminisce. She would describe each memory to me as if they were yesterday. I always listen intently, because I've learned more about the kind of person Therese was through the eyes of her mother than my own encounters with my cousin. There is an anger deep down in my aunt because of Therese's bout with cancer. Sometimes she wonders why she was able to beat it and her beautiful daughter did not. Why did God allow my aunt to stay and her child to go? We talk about this often, and we'll never know the answer, but who is really alive? I've asked my aunt if she feels better when she talks about Therese, and she said no. I've pondered on this for some time, but I see a joy in my aunt whenever she speaks about Therese; then, I watch her feel the loss all over again. When she reminisces the good times with Therese, we experience the glow her daughter left here. In those moments, my aunt leaves the darkness of her loneliness and loss behind, but she won't release her pain. For a long time, my aunt has been overcome with sorrow, and I hope that Therese's beauty and light heals her broken heart.

Therese's energy still permeates the physical in the places she's been and shared with others. I think Therese still shines bright, because her light is so constant, her memory lingers in the minds of all those who love her. She left a loving imprint, and it's a beautiful gift to the living. The cause is love and only love. While Therese was with us in this life, she shined in people's souls and left a lasting impression. This impression continues to make ripples of love through the people she has touched. She is still loved, and those she loved will always feel her love within.

Your Light

You were a light in the darkness,
A gift from high above,
An angel to nurture and care for
With unconditional love.
You were a spark in the embers
That inflamed a fire so bright,
Bringing warmth to the coldness of winter
And a light to the harsh, endless night.
This flame will forever be burning
In the hearts of those whom you've touched.
And though you've gone to our Maker,
You are valued ever as much.

I wanted to tell my aunt's story because it doesn't matter if a child is young or old if they pass away before their parents do. I think that this kind of loss may be the hardest to heal from. It's something one might not want to let go of.

My mother used to watch Mother Angelica on EWTN, and one day, I happened to come by while she was watching, and I heard Mother Angelica say, "Enjoy every miserable moment." It cracked me up, but later, I looked it up on the Internet and watched the whole segment. She was talking about living in the present moment. It was a wonderful broadcast, and I realized how many people continue to live in the worst moments of their lives. We can hold on to the sorrow, the trauma, the shock, the disbelief, the heartache, and the horror of a bad time. We fail to let it be over, we fail to let the moment pass, and we fail to move on. This part of grief is dangerous. We need to feel the present moment, then move on to the next moment. Maybe the next moment changes the course of our thinking. Maybe the new course of thinking helps us to grieve and let go. To be aware that we can get stuck is important to the process of healing.

> What do you do when nothing makes sense? It is the time for faith. One must grab onto God. One must be able to say, "I believe that God's goodness is going to bring about some greater good by this horror. It may not be a great good for me in this world, but it will be a great good someplace, somewhere, perhaps for those I love in the next world. (Fr. Benedict J. Groeschel, CFR)

People can tumble into a great darkness when their child passes away, and sorrow blinds what is true. Jesus promised eternal life through Him; therefore, death does not end life. This child is a light of love in the world, even after he or she is gone. This child, once again, is in God's infinite care. We are all children of God first, one body in Christ. Only God knows what's in store, so trust His wisdom in where He leads us. To believe in the promises of Christ is truly a saving grace.

We all suffer when a loved one is gone, but through my mourning, I have learned a lot about my faith. Catholicism is quite complex, but it has grounded me. The church is not the building or the politics of the religion. The church is the faithful. Therefore, I am never alone. All of our traditions are meant to incorporate faith into our daily lives and focus on God and all good things. I used to think that the Catholic church had too many rules, but I learned that all the rules assist me in following the two greatest commandments: to love God with all our heart, mind, and soul, and to love our neighbor as ourselves. If we love our neighbor as ourselves, we will do well by them. I have learned that if I follow these two rules, all the other rules of the Catholic church are followed by default.

Catholic traditions have kept me united and in community, but I had to actively seek God before I understood half of what is taught in catechism. You might be wondering why I'm bringing this up, but it's because my experiences with suffering are the same as my unique experiences with God. Everyone has their own way of thinking, and since I'm sharing my journey, I thought it would be beneficial to share my foundation. Love is my foundation, and it initiates all good things that heal. Suffering is a common thread in humanity, and I have discovered that God gives us the grace to get through all the storms in life. In my suffering, I learned of God's tremendous love for us. It humbles me. Catholics believe that through the Trinity, death does not hold us. God's divine mercy gave us Jesus Christ, a sacrifice in Himself, so that we could learn of His great love. God gave us life through Him, the Holy Spirit, which dwells within each of us. Can you imagine how much God loves us? Through the passion of Jesus Christ, we see darkness and suffering in full swing, and because of His example, we believe in resurrection, we believe in life after death, and we believe that God is with us always.

We must remember this in our time of grief, because then we know that our loved ones still have a place in our Creator's world, in the realm of His presence. Imagine the joy of coming home or being called back to paradise, home to perfect love. A child's life may be shorter than ours, but I believe God has set a place for them at His table of life. As for us, we are still pilgrims here on earth and should continue to live a life worthy of the love that was given to us. Let your deep love for your child strengthen you and guide you to become a person who lives beyond yourself. Your child was the face of God and will continue to feed your soul.

In God's Care

Mama, you were right! I had nothing to fear.
The Lord came and greeted me with infinite care.
His love touched my spirit and filled me with beauty.
It conquered my soul and called me to duty.
I know now my purpose was always to serve,
But without God beside me, I hadn't the nerve.
So He called me back home to do things up here,
To glorify His name and help everyone prepare.
I'm happier now; there's no pain and no crying,
Like when I was there feeling useless and dying.
Give thanks to Our Father because my suffering has subsided.
God makes my soul leap, and I'm always excited.
I'll see you again because your faith's in Our King.

Have hope in the promise the Almighty will bring.

Sanctuary

You were my sanctuary!
You rejuvenated me when I was weak,
You comforted me when I was sad,
You let me see that there was hope when I felt like giving up,
You loved me always, and that means the world to me.
I love you so much!
You were the only one that made me completely happy all my life.
I hope you know that you are very special.
Your work with me is all done now.
I thank you for every day.
But I thank God every day for you!

You Showed Your Love

Year after year, day after day,
You showed your love every possible way,
From teaching me to walk without any fear,
To cooking my meals or lending an ear.
You've patted my back with hope and with pride.
You held out your hands and stood by my side.
Through rain or shine or sleet or hail,
Your love has conquered and will always prevail.
Then came the time to heed God's call,
And I was summoned to His great hall.
My time with you was at an end.
In faith, you knew your heart would mend.
You showed your love unconditionally,
And your great reward is eternity.
Thank You.

My Anchor

You were my anchor in the crazy sea called life.
You held me steady in the waves of my emotions.
You kept me still when rough waters tried to capsize me.
You calmed the rocking of my wild soul.
You released me when the waters were calm.
You were my anchor.
The sea that was my life is no longer raging.
The current has carried me to safety.
My anchor has done its job.

God's Plan

Before God sent me down to earth, he
scanned the whole world through.
He looked for that one person that would aid my mission true,
And then he saw your heart and decided it was you.
He knew you'd be the one to nurture all my needs
And teach me all the things I need to plant and sow His seeds.
He knew you'd be the right one to eradicate the weeds.
So now I always thank the Lord for picking you for me
And for the foresight that He had to let you be the key.
I love you, Mom, and thank you for all you are to me!
Remember I am with you even if you can't see me
And that you've led me to Him through
your constant love and duty.
Have faith that I am free!

> Know that the Lord is God! It is He that
> made us, and we are His; we are His people, and
> the sheep of His pasture. (Psalms 100:3)

Part 4

Times of Celebration

The holidays are very difficult for people who are grieving. On the most joyous of occasions, we can fall desperately into sorrow because we have lost the company of a person that has made a deep impact on our lives. We feel the loss most especially during the holidays. How can we celebrate when they are gone?

The answer is that we should celebrate the fact that they are with our Holy Father on the "holy" days. They are in His awesome presence. They are no longer in pain, no longer worried, no longer in need. They no longer are bound to the ways of the world. They are with our Creator and are free from the burdens of this earth, so we should celebrate their freedom instead of being sad.

We may miss them more, but we should acknowledge where they are and be happy for them. It is sad for us, and it is hard not to feel sorry for ourselves, but pray for help. God will take care of our needs if we only ask. If you are finding it hard to find the right words, there are many websites and prayers online that can help with prayer and meditation. True conversation with God comes from your heart. Express your sadness, your anger, your fear, and any emotions you are feeling while you pray. The Lord understands and will help you through.

The supreme test of our confidence in God
lies, perhaps, in those moments of complete

inner darkness in which we feel as though we are
forsaken by God. (Dietrich von Hildebrand)

Like anything in the world, grief is temporary. It might not
feel like you have any control over what is or has happened, but you
have the power to hold on to your grief or let it go. You have a right
to feel whatever you are feeling just as you have a right to move forward and away from the sadness, if that is your choice. The holidays
usually hold special memories for people. Birthdays, anniversaries,
Christmas, New Years, Easter, and all those celebrated times bring
people together in celebration and joy. I encourage you to rejoice in
the memories of these times with your departed loved one. It is in joy
that love persists with passion beyond the night.

Wherever I have lived, I have found something truly amazing
about the shadows of the place. I've always known beauty, but this is
because of my perception. When I travel to work, I travel over hills
toward the west. The sun is behind me in the mornings, and the
shadows constantly change the look of the terrain. The appearance of
the landscape is always changing even if everything is still in the same
place. The view, whether in the light or shadows, is always pretty,
but the light tends to draw me. When the sky is overcast, the energy
seems gloomy, but if I choose to view things with hope beyond the
clouds, my perception of my surroundings still brings me joy and
hope of warmth and sunshine.

In the dark, we see nothing. In the light, we see everything. In
the shadows, we see some things, and other things are hidden, so we
see partial. Our human nature sees in the shadows and often causes
us to assume. We really don't know anything about the afterlife. It
is a mystery, but hope springs forth through faith. The holidays are
holy days of mystery and hope. They are days celebrating triumph
over evil, triumph over diversity, and triumph over tyranny. Let the
holidays be your triumph over grief. Remember the joy, remember
the love, and remember that hope springs eternal.

On Your Birthday

Today you came into the world and blessed us for a while.
You had a way about you that always made us smile.
Although you've gone to heaven's gate, we're thinking of you still
And praying for you always. We love you, birthday girl!
Oh, thank you for your prayers; they fill a precious hole, for
through You and heartfelt prayers, the Lord restores my soul.
I love you, friends and family. I know how much you care.
It fills me full of joy to know that soon we'll meet up here.

Celebrate the New Year

Oh fireworks, oh fireworks,
How beautiful your glow.
I see your sparkling brilliance from my cloud.
Your festive lights shine through the night
To celebrate the year.
Up here, in heaven, trumpets sound aloud.
Oh celebrate, just celebrate.
Leave saddened hearts behind.
Rejoice for me because I feel your love.
And as this year comes to a close
Be rid of all your tears.
I promise I am watching from above.
The Father, Son, and Holy Ghost
Can make your burdens light.
Just trust His will so you can start anew.
Through faith and hope, but mostly love,
Your prayers raised me up.
My spirit, now, will always be with you.
In jubilee, I ask of you,
Rejoice with a full heart,
With angels, I am greeting this New Year.
And every time you reminisce,
Your voice will call to me,
And love will always guide my spirit there!

Oh, Saint Patrick

Oh, Saint Patrick, on your day
I hope and wish that people pray
For luck to come our mission's way
And for God to bless the paths we lay.
Oh, Saint Patrick, strong and clear,
Help us vanquish deep despair.
Let the lost know we are here
To light their dark and believe we care.
Oh, Saint Patrick, help them see
The clover's beautiful Trinity.
And through this hope-filled charity
Gather us in unity.

Saint Valentine

Saint Valentine, we give a cry,
For love that's lost but never dies.
As Christ ignites our hearts to love,
Pray we release our pain enough
To see the fire that still does burn
And heals our soul that now does mourn.

Valentine's Wish

Here's a Valentine's wish for you:
To love each other as families do,
With faith, forgiveness, kindness, and care,
For love is undying, no gift can compare.
Show sweet little gestures and do what you can
To strengthen your bonds and ripples expand.
I promise it'll help to make life content
When love is unconditionally sent.

Thanksgiving

I'm at a feast at the Table of Plenty.
I dine with the Bread of Life.
I'm rejoicing with Jesus, my savior,
The splendor of His majesty rife.
The beauty of this table
Is unlike I've ever seen.
It is blessed with nothing lacking,
Places set with spotless gleam.
I'm surrounded by saints and angels,
A heavenly sound of praise.
A light that fills the core of my soul
Comes lovingly from His gaze.
I'll give thanks with all of my being
For the lessons I've learned from you.
God welcomed me into His kingdom,
Because the source of your love was true.
He used you as a catapult
To draw me into grace,
And from your life, I saw the Lord,
For God had shown His face.

It's Easter Time

It's Easter time and spring is here,
A time for new life, true hope, and good cheer.
Here in heaven, the choir speaks straight to your heart
And joy fills the air even though we're apart.
It's a time to be with those we hold dear.
Don't miss me too much; in spirit, I'm there.
I know you're unhappy when you can't touch or feel me.
Just believe with your heart what your eyes cannot see.
The day of Christ's rising is such an occasion.
Celebrate, and be happy in wondrous elation.
On Easter Day, Jesus Christ set us free.
Hope springs eternal, so rejoice gleefully.

Celebrating Easter

Chocolate bunnies, Easter eggs, and baskets full of fun.
I'll send you cool breezes and marshmallow
clouds before the day is done.
We'll celebrate the rising of man's Savior and God's son.
I'll rejoice up here in heaven; you'll rejoice in the warmth of the sun.
I'll send you a beautiful rainbow just so you know I care.
Just pretend it's a special gift that all of us can share.
Be happy on this joyful day even if I'm absent there.
You'll be spending Easter on earth; I'll be spending Easter up here.
I'll chase away the gray clouds so you'll have a beautiful day
For barbecues, activities, and children fun at play.
You'll celebrate this Easter the fun traditional way.
I'll celebrate this Easter the beautiful heavenly way.

Celebrating Mother's Day

A mother's love is tender, unconditional, and true.
Today's a day to celebrate the brilliant wonder of you.
Your forgiveness is a blessing, your discipline is just.
I know that your whole life has been centered on us.
I'm celebrating your beauty with my heavenly friends above
And rejoicing in the magic that is coming from your love.
It surrounds me every moment because it
comes straight from your heart.
Your care surpasses all the bounds that keep us far apart.
Every day you visit me to let me know you're there,
But let me tell you, Mama, that I am everywhere.
All the places that we've been to hold a memory,
I hope your grief will never blind the things your heart should see.
Therefore, Happy Mother's Day, dear
Mom, I love and miss you too.
Know that with the angels and saints, I'm celebrating you!

Father's Day in Heaven

Father's Day in heaven is quite spectacular.
I feel like an infant wrapped in his arms.
His love engulfs the very core of my being.
He surrounds me with tenderness and care.
The music of his angels pierces my heart with arrows of beauty.
The light of saintly prayers sparkle and shine
like the stars in a clear night sky.
He is truth, He is hope, He is joy, He is Love.
Happy Father's Day!

Celebrating Father's Day

Today I'm in our Father's hands; he holds me close in safety.
I feel loved, I feel secure, I am at peace.
Today in wonderful delight, we celebrate our fathers
With exalted joy, in loving truth, with perfect grace.
I celebrate this Father's Day with the heavenly Father of all.
I know joy, I know truth, I know love.

Heavenly Christmas

I see my earthly paradise sparkling down below.
From my perch from high above, it's as bright as heaven's glow.
The angels sit here with me and tell me that it's nice
That I'm celebrating in heaven the birth of Jesus Christ.
I hear the sounds of Christmas sung in joy and voices raised,
But nothing can compare with this choir's songs of praise.
Their voices are so mystic and exalt our newborn King.
It pierces deep inside the soul to hear the angels sing.
I know you really miss me, and I seem so far away,
But please be happy that I'm here with Jesus on his birthday.
Offer up a prayer or two, and send it high above.
The greatest gift that we can give is unconditional love.
Remember Jesus taught us how to love through all his stories.

I've learned that it's the reason He's the King of endless glory.
He spread his love unselfishly while he was down on earth,
So do the same, and give your love not only on his birth.
I'll always be there with you, even if I'm not at home,
But I'm sharing a heavenly Christmas with the Holy Father's Son.

Part 5

Life or Death

The Midnight Hour

Midnight, the end of a day or the beginning of a new day. Some might interpret it as the middle of night, the darkest hour, the center of darkness. How we interpret things truly makes a difference in how we deal with situations and what kind of impact the situation makes on us. This, in turn, makes an impact on those around us. Midnight, to me now, is not just the ending of a day but the beginning of a new one. This change of perception changed my entire life and transformed me into a more productive and positive person. I thank God that I started seeing the light!

There was a long period of my life when midnight seemed like the darkest hour. Depression was my midnight, and its darkness seemed to engulf my whole being. Darkness and light cannot share the same space, so I couldn't see anything as they truly were. All the evils in my life surrounded me, and I was in a very lonely place. Every morning, I struggled to find a reason to get up. Most days, I would pull the covers over my head, go back to sleep, and dread the time I'd have to physically get up. When I got out of bed, a hundred little demons would jump on my back, and their burden weighed me down. My thoughts ran to things like these: Why did I have to get up? I wish I wasn't here. Why am I here? I wonder what would happen if I died. No one would miss me if I disappeared. What is the purpose of living? I wish I was never born. Each step was physically difficult and painful. Everything was shadowed in gloom, and I couldn't see any beauty or feel any joy. The pain in my chest was like my heart being squeezed tight in a fist and held captive. I couldn't even find the cause of why I felt this way. It was extreme sadness and complete disappointment in myself. This perception had two consequences: I found fault in the people in my life most of the time, and I despised everything I was doing.

There was no particular reason why I was so unhappy. I didn't even know what would make me happy. No one could see my sadness, because I hid it well. I lied, and I always had a smile on my face when people saw me. Then I subtly started to disengage. I kept myself unavailable to socialize. My conversations became shallow and I avoided subjects that pertained to my personal life. I didn't want people to notice me. This was a big telltale of where I was emotionally and spiritually, because before I was depressed, I was very social. Some people used to call me a social butterfly, because I talked to everyone about anything.

My life was a mess, and I was a mess for a very long time. My life wasn't bad by any means. Some people would say I had a really good and easy life. I just didn't find any satisfaction in the life I was living. I wasn't living with purpose. Again, there wasn't a justifiable reason for feeling this way. From a young age, I thought that if I had a good job, got married, had children, and had good friends, I'd be happy. I didn't have children, but I had everything else, and I was not happy!

In the Shadows

On sunny days, I'm in the shadows hiding from its shine.
When someone asks if I'm all right, I always say I'm fine.
I go about my business and hardly make a sound,
Even when the family is gathering around.
I disappear into the corners and stay out of their sight
And hope that no one notices when I go into the night.

I feel so insignificant and don't know the reason why.
I cannot find the energy in life to really try.
I've tried to talk to others about how I truly feel,
But the response I always seem to get doesn't really heal.
So I step into the shadows and hide my heart's deep fear
And hope that no one notices when I choose to disappear.

Life really didn't make sense to me. I didn't believe that I was important. I didn't think I mattered. I couldn't see the affect my life had on others, and it didn't matter. All of my relationships suffered because of what I thought. I didn't contact my family or my good friends. I never attended mass during this time. I was really lost in self-pity and disgusted with the circumstances I had trapped myself in. I was in an unhappy marriage and unfulfilling job and had no hope of a bright future. Everything I did was acceptable, but there was no joy.

I felt trapped, I felt devalued, and I felt worthless. I couldn't offer anything to society, and I wasn't contributing at all to humanity. My soul kept sinking deeper and deeper into a void that couldn't be filled by anything. I didn't have a purpose, my goals dissipated, and I started to hate myself. I couldn't understand why I was so miserable. I had a decent life by society's standards, but when I was depressed, I wouldn't acknowledge anything good. I knew that purpose gives one hope, that goals give motivation, and that healthy relationships fill a void, but my mental state prevented me from knowing I had a purpose, and I felt it was useless to create goals for myself. I couldn't contribute to a healthy relationship, because I couldn't even relate to myself and what I wanted. I was misguided by the darkness of my thoughts.

This dark time was all about me and what caused my misery. Sometimes I'd feel overwhelmed with all of life's complications. I had depended on others to fill those empty spaces. I needed work and responsibilities to make me feel valuable. Then I discovered that when I depended on these things, those spaces of emptiness in my soul could never be filled. The second greatest commandment is to love our neighbors as ourselves, so in this period of my life, love was not present in my heart.

I discovered, after many years of unhappiness, that love, rather Godly love, was the only cure for my longing. I had to learn how to see myself through the eyes of my creator. What was there to love? I thought I was nothing, and I wasn't worthy of God's love. I wasn't humble at this time, and my attitude was not pretty. This was a long journey, but it became my most valued lesson in life. In my pursuit of happiness, I did not follow a path that was utilizing my natural gifts and talents. None of my endeavors touched the desires of my heart. I was not really fulfilled with what I was doing or with what I had, because my soul was always longing for something else. I was stuck. In this period of despair, I could not see God's will for me. I couldn't see the purpose I was meant to fulfill in my life, because my face was turned away from the Lord. I was weak, and I didn't notice that Jesus had His arms open wide for me on that cross. I didn't even have a desire to change.

In this section, I talk about suicide and my own experiences with it. I hope that what I have gone through helps in your journey as well. If you are depressed or have suffered from the effects of suicide, know that you are not alone.

> Two are better than one, because they have a good reward for their toil. For if they fall, one will lift up his fellow; but woe to him who is alone when he falls and has not another to lift him up. Again, if two lie together, they are warm; but how can one be warm alone? And though a man might prevail against one who is alone, two will withstand him. A threefold cord is not quickly broken. (Ecclesiastes 4:9–12)

Let Me In

I see you standing there all alone,
Living life without a friend.
Oh, how can I ever make you believe
I will love you 'til the end.

Call on me to walk by your side.
Ask of me, and I'll be your guide.
Ever faithful, ever true,
I promise I will never leave you.
You are my child forever.
I'll always listen when you share.
If you invite me into your life,
You'll see how much I really care.
Just lean on me, and take my hand.
Be with me. I'll help you stand.
I am the beginning and the end.
You will not be alone ever again.

Unfortunately, society tends to promote things that only bring temporary happiness. If we own a nice car, nice clothes, or a dream home, we are supposed to be happy. If we have a job that is satisfying and pays a lot, we will be happy. If we have prestige or fame, we will be happy. If we have a partner, we will be happy. But our happiness does not come from outside sources. Happiness must come from within. Everything tangible can be lost, taken away, stolen, or destroyed, but the soul can find joy in moments of love, mercy, and giving. Our value must be known to ourselves first, and we must know that we are important in this world, regardless of our status. Every person makes a ripple and therefore affects the world. Depression, despondency, and despair camouflages a person's worth.

Chains of My Making

Weighed by the chains of my own making,
Lord, I turn to thee.
Only You can lift my burdens.
Only You can set me free.
Forgive me for my boastfulness,
My unrelenting role.
Forgive me for my selfish ways.
Have mercy on my soul.

I know that every sin committed
Hung Jesus on that wood.
Oh, Lord, I ask forgiveness
For not living as I should.
Teach me to be a humble servant,
One who'll love like You.
Help me to be a real example
Of living in the truth.

Pray for Me

He whispered to me, "Your life is worthless,
put down your shield, and come with me."
My Lord stepped in and firmly stated,
"You are my child, can't you see?"
I cried with tears of joy and sadness,
not knowing where to ease my pain.
Then Jesus said, in loving kindness,
"Do not take your life in vain.
I have many plans for you, and Satan is a liar!
Remember how I died for you?
I saved you from hell's fire.
I was ridiculed and rejected.
I had to wear a crown of thorns.
I was spit upon and hated.
My heart was truly torn.
I even asked my Father
Why I had been forsaken.
He told me joy would cometh
After I was taken.
Satan deceives the weary soul
And fills you full of doubt,
But if you choose to end your life,
You'll have no chance to win your bout.
Believe in me, my child,
For through me, you are saved.

My love is never-failing,
And your road is carefully paved."
But in that darkened hour
As I heard my Father speak,
The devil took advantage
And ended life for me.
The Holy Spirit saved me
And put me all alone
So I could contemplate my life
And know where I belong.
Every time you speak of me
Is a beautiful sounding prose,
And every prayer said for me
Is aroma to my nose.
Your thoughts and prayers will raise me up,
Because they're filled with love.
They help me to submit myself
So I can rise above.

When I was still with my ex-husband, we sold our house and moved into his sister's duplex. His niece, Joy, lived next door. Joy and I became very close. Misery loves company, and we were both pretty unhappy at that time. She was the only one I would confide in about my problems and how I truly felt. She seemed to be able to relate to my feelings, but we fed each other's woes. We would often sit in the front carport and talk. She listened to my complaints and gave me advice. I listened to hers and gave her advice. But our advice to each other was not sound advice. We tended to redirect the responsibility of our misery to the people we lived with or were constantly around. She made it possible to ignore the problem and just get on with life. I thought she was so strong and wise for her age, because I always felt better after we talked. She was only twenty-five.

One day I argued with her uncle, and I was so angry that I started walking down the street. She must have sensed some kind of danger, because I was thinking of hanging myself. She ran to me and asked me not to do anything stupid and not to hurt myself. She told me that I was important to her and to my family and friends. I promised that I wouldn't do anything drastic and then walked to a cemetery close by. It might seem like a weird thing to do, but as soon as I entered that hallowed ground, I calmed down and went to my in-laws' grave sites and started to pray. I had an urge to say the rosary. I said the sorrowful mysteries, and it was very powerful in that moment. My meditation went something like this:

- In the name of the Father, the Son, and the Holy Spirit: I called on the Trinity to bless my mind, my heart, and my entire being.
- The Apostle's Creed: I asked God to help my unbelief.
- The Lord's Prayer: I started to cry when I came to the part that says, "And forgive us our trespasses." I wanted to take my life.
- Three Hail Marys: I asked for an increase of faith, hope, and love. I asked the Blessed Mother to teach me how to pray.
- The first sorrowful mystery, the Agony in the Garden: Jesus is in the Garden of Gethsemane contemplating the task before Him. He knows of the suffering He is about to endure and sweats. He worries and asks God to be released from the passion but is so submissive to the will of God that he gracefully accepts it for the love of mankind. Jesus suffered in His heart and soul for what worries all of us. I started thinking about why I was worried and how it compared to Jesus. I realized how selfish and silly I was being and was sorry. I was still crying.
- The second sorrowful mystery, the Scourging at the Pillar: Jesus was found guiltless and was physically assaulted for no reason. His body suffered tremendously, because He was beaten beyond recognition. I thought, *Why?* I cried even more, because I wanted to end my life that wasn't even in any physical pain.
- The third sorrowful mystery, the Crowning with Thorns: Jesus is mocked and ridiculed. I wondered about who was

mocking and ridiculing me. I was the only one I could think of that was putting me down. How stupid I've been to think my problems were not solvable.

- The fourth sorrowful mystery, the Carrying of the Cross: Jesus carried this heavy cross to His death, being whipped and laughed at. Nobody came to His defense, and here I was inviting death. I thought about Joy and how she ran after me, telling me she loved me to stop me from hurting myself. I realized how ridiculous my thinking had been. Still crying, I asked Jesus to forgive me with my whole heart.

- The fifth sorrowful mystery, the Crucifixion: Jesus dies on the cross. Death, that's what I thought. I realized how permanent it was and started to think about who would be affected by my death. My mother immediately came to my mind and remembered her unconditional love for me. How could I be so selfish and not think about my family? I was so sorry for my actions, my inactions, my words, and my thoughts.

- Hail Holy Queen: I asked Mary to pray for me, and then I calmed down and felt the love of God come over me.

It was a beautiful revelation! This contemplation opened my eyes to something bigger than me. This was what I was searching for—God's love! I found it in my despair, on my knees, on hallowed ground, in a cemetery surrounded by death, and in that place, I found true life.

Joy had caught me in my despair and knew I needed my family who loved me. She called my mother when I was at the cemetery; although, she had no idea where I was. My mother called my brothers and sisters, and they all came looking for me. Joy showed me love at the perfect time and knew me well enough to catch me in my lowest moment. The Lord converted me that day and called me to a life in servitude to *love*.

Joy was a beautiful person, inside and out. She always put others first, and she seemed to have a positive view on things. She never failed in showing how she cared for her friends and family. We talked a lot, and after our talks, she always left me hopeful. It always came across that she didn't let anything really bother her.

She was actually struggling with difficult family matters at that time but always gave me the impression that she knew the problems would all work themselves out. One day, she was telling me about the reality TV shows she liked watching, mostly crime investigations. She commented on how certain shows taught people how to do bad things correctly and without being caught. She was telling me that they taught people how to kill, how to commit robberies, which kinds of death are the most painless, and the like. I was wondering how we got on the subject and asked her, but she just said it was interesting to her. She mentioned these shows during several conversations after my cemetery incident. I should have been suspicious, but I was oblivious.

About two weeks later, her uncle and I were going to a movie. Joy was outside, and I asked her if she wanted to come with us. She declined but asked if she could use my car to go to a party later. I said yes and gave her the keys. When we were leaving for the show, Joy pulled my car to the side of the house, and I thought that was really odd. She said she was going to wash it before she went to the party, but I wondered why she didn't just wash it in the carport. My husband also found it odd, but we were getting late for the movie and left. It was on the back of my mind on our way home and when we pulled into the carport, I had a very, very bad feeling. My car was still at the side, and it was running with Joy in the driver's seat apparently sleeping.

The car was locked. I knocked lightly on the window, but she didn't respond. At first, I thought she was ignoring me because she had a rosary in her hand, and I thought she might be praying, but she didn't move. I knocked harder and yelled her name, but still no response. My husband checked the doors, went to the other side of the car, yelled for me to call 911, and told me to stand back. She had jury rigged a water hose into the car from the muffler. He bashed in the back window while I called 911; then, he opened the doors. She had the air-conditioning faced to her, and her body was cold. We pulled Joy out of the car. Her knees were still warm. I handed him the phone while I checked her. She wasn't breathing, so I began CPR. I remember thinking that since her knees were still warm when we pulled her out of the car, she had a chance, so I would breathe for her and pump her heart until the medics came. Then they would revive her. The ambulance came and took her to the hospital. We followed and called her family.

I was crying in the waiting room when her brothers came in. Her mother was in Korea visiting Joy's younger sister, so we hadn't called her yet. Joy was still with the doctors for what it seemed like an eternity. I didn't know what to say to her family or how to say anything at all. The doctor came out of the room and told us Joy was dead. They had tried everything they could to revive her, but she had suffocated from hypoxia caused by carbon monoxide poisoning.

My husband had to call his sister to tell her the dreadful news. After that, the blame game began. Everyone started blaming each other. There were so many unanswered questions. We all felt we knew the reason, and we all felt "it wasn't me." We also felt we could have done something to prevent it. We were angry, we were guilty, we were sorry, but none of us took responsibility for our inaction or lack of concern for her problems. Then we were self-righteous, judgmental, embarrassed, and ashamed. The anger was harsh. Everyone was angry at each other, but mostly at Joy. How could she be so selfish as to take her life away from us? I understood her motives, but I couldn't understand why the Holy Spirit didn't save her the way He saved me.

> But I call upon God; and the Lord will save
> me. (Psalms 55:16)

The support her family received during the nightly rosaries was greatly needed. Much like when my father died, the friendship and stories helped in healing, and the preparations helped in coping. The difference was that as people gathered to pray for Joy, they always asked the family those dreaded questions, "Why?" and "What happened?" Those questions still remain unanswered. How could such a loving soul become so hopeless? I should have been able to answer this question because death had been on my mind too, but I couldn't! Regardless of all of this, Joy's life and death affected the lives of so many people. She loved while she was here, and we had to come to terms with the fact that we will never know why she chose to leave us. Her life and death have made many ripples in the lives of those who knew her. I have never thought of taking my life again, and I finally had the courage to change my life and my thinking.

Humble my heart, O Lord, that I may see past the pain so deeply etched in it. Heal the scars that open with every thought of (name). I thought (name) was fine. I feel responsible, but I know I am not. Why wasn't our love enough to make (name) want to stay with us? Were we too hard on her or him? Did my rejection have anything to do with this suicide? Help me to understand this. I can't get over my anger, and I feel (name) had no right to do this! Grant me the grace to forgive, and please grant me the gifts of knowledge and understanding. Humble me that I might not curse (name) but be able to pray for him or her with mercy. Please forgive me for my ill thoughts and for my selfishness. I am hurt, and I humbly ask You to heal me. Amen

After everything came to an end, the rosaries and the funeral, some of Joy's close friends and I formed a nonprofit organization called the April Joy Foundation to bring awareness to the problem of suicide. We started a support group and collaborated with social services and private entities for counseling and support. I met so many people who had dealt with suicide, and even if the circumstances were different, we all vividly remember how we felt with this person during their lifetime. I learned that nobody is worthless! Every life is formed for love, to love, and to be loved. In forming this foundation, we all learned so much about the problems associated with suicide and depression. It was unfounded to have seen the devastation suicide causes families and individuals and for how long the effect lasts. The tasks I had made me look at my life, and I started to see purpose again, even as I mourned Joy.

I was really angry at Joy! I thought she was a hypocrite because she stopped me when I wanted to end it all; then, she went ahead and did it! She made me realize that my life was not mine to take but mine to give. I went to confession and was telling my priest everything that I was thinking about Joy and how it was so difficult to forgive her. During the sacrament of reconciliation, there is a time of counseling. I asked him about suicide, and He explained that the church's position on suicide. He said we are not sure if that person, in that last moment of their life, repented and asked God forgiveness. We are not sure of or responsibility for the relationship or lack of relationship one has with God. It is free will, but we can advise and lead them by example and try to draw them into grace through love. He explained about purgatory again and advised me not to judge, because that is God's right alone. We can only continue to love this person and offer up prayers for them. This comforted me and gave me the grace to forgive.

I forgave her, I forgave myself, I forgave, and that was my first step toward healing. I delve into prayer, the Bible, and religion again. Only through the beautiful Trinity of the Father, the Son, and the Holy Spirit have I gained a peaceful mind and a full heart. Through the Holy Spirit, I received grace and all that I needed to overcome my sadness and heartache. God always provides. I've learned through all of my experiences that trust in God is very important but also very difficult to do. It requires complete faith in the Divine, but we choose it.

> Being unwanted, unloved, uncared for, forgotten by everybody…I think that is a much greater hunger, a much greater poverty than a person who has nothing to eat. (St. Teresa of Calcutta)

Could I Have Changed Things

As the sun rises in the sky,
I can't help but wonder and ask if and why.
Why you left me in gloom's dark hour?
Why you took with you my power?
Why do I dread the new day's dawn?
Why can't I accept that you're really gone?

If I'd been there, could I have saved you?
If you talked to me, would I have a clue?
Did I love you enough when you were living?
Could I have changed why your heart was grieving?
Could I have stopped you from taking your life?
Why couldn't you overcome your heartache and strife?
I want to forgive you, but it's hard when I'm mad.
See, you left me here so hurt and sad.
I love you so deeply and want you here.
The weight on my heart is too heavy to bear.
When the sun sets every day,
I sit alone and lovingly pray.
I pray God makes my heart feel light
And makes me strong enough to fight.
I pray you feel my love inside.
I pray this pain in my soul will subside.
I pray God forgives us, both you and me,
And that he grants us serenity.
Please know I loved you with all my heart
And continue to love you even though we're apart.

Are we responsible for the choices of others? No, but we are responsible for our actions or inactions of love. Compassion, forgiveness, and kindness are acts of love. Prayer is an act of love. Mercy is love in action, and we must be merciful during this life. We can only control our actions and inactions, how we respond, or how unresponsive we are, in any given situation.

Sometimes we get so busy, trying to finish all the things we've set out to do that day that we might just overlook the needs of others. Sometimes we get so preoccupied with our own business that we forget to smile or to extend simple courtesies to others. Sometimes we don't see that someone needs us. It is natural to seek happiness in our relationships, in our work, and in our surroundings, but to some, happiness always seems to escape their grasp, and the hardness of the world hits them full force. Peace is not obtainable, and the feelings of despair start to play havoc on the soul. Society can be cruel and harsh, and that reality can be devastating. We need to be aware, and we need to do our part!

If you have lost someone to suicide, I am heartily sorry for your loss. It is time to release them from your sadness, from your anger, from your guilt, from your pain. If you love them, pray for them. If you miss them, hold fast to the love they gave you. They are now in the hands of the Lord, and He will take care of them. Turn to God.

On the day I cried out, you answered me,
my strength of soul you increased. (Psalms 138:3)

I'm Sorry

I'm sorry that I didn't see
The care and love you held for me.
I'm sorry that I took my life
And caused more sadness and more strife.
I'm sorry I couldn't see the day.
Instead, the darkness hid my way.
I'm sorry I couldn't escape my despair.
Pride kept me from carrying the cross I should bear.
I'm sorry for hiding away from your kindness
And for being selfish, which caused my blindness.
I'm sorry for not opening my eyes.
Satan was dressed in a sheep's disguise.
I'm sorry my faith was lost in the storm,
And that it left you grieving and torn.
I'm sorry I rejected the path laid for me,
And that I left you in such misery.
I'm sorry I did not love you enough
To stand up and fight when life got tough.
I'm sorry I gave up, and although I'd be free,
I'm heartily sorry. Please, please forgive me.

People deal with hardships in many ways. Some people cope, some despair, and some become despondent. We never know how a single individual responds to the situations in their lives or the rejections they may feel. We can only assume we know how a person will respond by their overall character and personality. I've learned, through the loss of people I've cared about, that we only know a part of a person's character by what they reveal to us or how they react to us, so we don't really know how anybody is going to cope with different situations unless we are directly involved. We can assume, but we may be wrong. Usually people will talk about what is bothering them, but many keep their troubles hidden. A person who is often bubbly and happy can hide their turmoil behind a smile but will hint that something is wrong or bothering them. A person whom we might assume is very strong may in fact be hiding their weakness behind their feistiness. A person who is comical may hide loneliness behind their jokes. We can only guess through subtle hints that a person is in real trouble. Pride plays a part also. Not very many people want to admit that they are struggling inside. We are taught that the strong survive, so we act strong. Some people, even those we love, might feel that the only escape from their troublesome life is death.

I have known too many people that have chosen death over life. Joy was just the first of these stories. Several were kind, funny, beautiful, and outwardly happy people. Each situation was different, each was from a different age group, each in a different stage of their lives, but I never thought any of them would give up on life. They may have given subtle signs of their despair, but I never noticed because the problems they faced may have seemed solvable to me. Suicide is a darkness no one can explain.

When someone commits suicide, there are so many unanswered questions, and it is natural to be angry at that person. We feel that he or she had no right to take their life away from us, and we always ask, "Why?" Closure does not always come with understanding, but it does come with forgiveness. Forgiveness lightens the weight that sits on our shoulders and releases the burdens strapped on our backs by the pain and uncertainty that stems from anger.

Suicidal thoughts are not stereotyped. They can pass through the minds of anyone for any reason, and we should be aware of them.

When depression hits, it feels like an eagle's talons are hooked in the heart. It seems as though God has abandoned us, but the Spirit is always with us, watching and waiting for us to rely completely on God. The Spirit patiently waits for us to humble ourselves to providence. When we turn to God in faith and humility and deeply believe that we are loved, a great burden is lifted from our soul. It is refreshed and strengthened anew. If you've dealt with suicide, don't blame yourself! It is not yours to claim.

All we can do in this lifetime is love each other and try our best to open our arms to those in despair. We can encourage each other to be an expression of love. We can build each other up to be good citizens of good character. We can inspire joyful service by being examples of humility in charity. Works of mercy don't buy our way to heaven, but they teach us how to love properly by becoming a part of our character through habit. God made us to love.

> Before I formed you in the womb I knew you, and before you were born I consecrated you; I appointed you a prophet to the nations. (Jeremiah 1:5)

I have found that the purpose for my life is not for myself, but for others. I am valued by others and have affected others with my love and care. My worth is from God and nothing else. For whatever reason, I was created. I was put here on earth to use my gifts and talents to bring people to an active love. Now I know I fell into depression because I was not being whom God intended me to be. I never made use of the natural talents and gifts I was given to serve others. When we don't allow the Holy Spirit to work through us, there is a great work that is not done in the world, so our soul grieves. Mine was grieving. Once I said *yes*, grace was mine. God granted me the grace to see and to act. Jesus became my teacher and continually teaches me how to love, especially myself.

> You formed my inmost being; you knit me in my mother's womb. I praise you, because I am

wonderfully made; wonderful are your works!
My very self you know. (Psalms 139:13–14)

Grief has many faces. It is associated with death, but one of its faces is depression. Depression can hit a person, any person, out of the blue. It can also be caused by a chemical imbalance. Sometimes it is caused by circumstances, sometimes it's the environment, but it is always emotional. Overcoming grief contributes to strength, courage, faith, and hope. Just as grief has many faces, so does God. Society has taught us to judge people by their success, but fulfillment comes from moments that touch our soul, moments of mercy, moments of love.

God shows His face in the downtrodden, the lowly, the heart-broken, and the like. Our downfall is that, in our busy day-to-day activities, we fail to see them. In these faces, we have opportunities to practice mercy and to live humbly. The paradigm is that as we are able to see the faces of God in these people; God shows His face to these people in you.

Every person is unique, but we are all affected by the choices we make and the views we choose. Suicide cannot be categorized by any "type" of personality. We cannot tell who are most prone to take their lives. I wish we could know, because then it would be easier to recognize the symptoms. Unfortunately, suicide is random and com-mitted by all types of personalities. It is not a weakness, nor a trait, it is not even just a situation. It might be a combination of factors, but we can never categorize it, because the ones who've committed suicide are gone and cannot tell us their stories. We will never know the exact cause of why someone makes that choice, but we can open ourselves up to loving those around us.

We can release the shame, the guilt, the unanswered questions, and the anger. We can let go of the responsibility of their choice. We can still love them and remember the moments they shared with us. We can rejoice in the gift of time spent together in laughter and sometimes tears. We can forgive them, and we can forgive ourselves.

I will refresh the weary and satisfy the faint.
(Jeremiah 31:25)

Only God knows what's in our hearts, but He tells each of us what we are supposed to do and how we are supposed to treat others. We are called to love. We are made to love.

In everything we do, we should be aware that a person in our midst might need our love. God gives us gifts and talents to show charity to those around us. Everyone can use a smile, a gentle hand, a shoulder to cry on, and a willing friendship. Everyone needs to know that they are worth loving, that they are important, that they can make an impact, that they are valuable in life. Letting them know is an act of love and kindness.

> Let us always meet each other with a smile,
> for the smile is the beginning of love. (St. Teresa
> of Calcutta)

Answers do not always bring peace, but peace always comes with faith. I wrote these poems after Joy's death, and you can see how angry and confused I was. It's not wrong to feel these emotions. I loved Joy, she was my friend, she was my confidante, and she was beautiful. At one point, I felt guilty for feeling the way I was feeling, but it was all part of the healing process. I finally came to terms with everything, and I forgave. Then I released all the sadness, and I healed. I encourage you again to go through your emotions and release them through your gifts.

How Do I Let You Go

How can I let you go when the curse of
how you left me haunts my mind?
How can my heart heal when all my
questions were left unanswered?
How will my soul be free when you left my heart tangled with guilt?
How do I let you go?
Where can I find all the answers I seek to
ease this pounding in my brain?

Should I even look when the cause of your
death blinds me with rage?
Will my anger subside if all the answers came or will it increase?
How do I let you go?

What, When, Why, and How

What were you thinking when you took your life away?
What could I have done to make you want to stay?
What made life so bad that you couldn't stand and fight?
What made you believe that you even had the right?
When did you start feeling that your life wasn't worth much?
When did you lose hope and give death its final clutch?
When did you stop thinking that we didn't love you so?
When did pride convince you not to let your feelings show?
Why did you abandon us without leaving us a clue?
Why did you believe that we would never miss you?
Why did fate allow you to make this fatal choice?
Why couldn't you hear the echo of God's loving voice?
How could you just leave us without letting us know?
How are we supposed to accept the fact that you wanted to go?
How do we cope with your loss without any answers to why?
How do we forgive you and finally say, "Goodbye"?

I Must Forgive

I must forgive; I must forgive.
Because I love you, I must forgive.
I must forgive; I must forgive.
To be released, I must forgive.
I must forgive; I must forgive.
To let you go, I must forgive.
I must forgive; I must forgive.
To heal the pain, I must forgive.
I must forgive; I must forgive.
To be at peace, I must forgive.

I must forgive; I must forgive.
To be forgiven, I must forgive.
I must forgive; I must forgive.
To live again, I must forgive.

Heavenly Father, I need you. I am so weak and full of sorrow. Give me strength, oh Lord, to get through this time. My grief and my guilt overwhelm me. I have doubt, and I am so angry at this person for taking his or her own life. Please help me to forgive him or her for doing this. I need your help to let him or her go. Please, Father, take him or her into your care and bless me with the humility to let you take over. I ask you to remove doubt from my heart and to help me overcome my guilt and my grief. I know you are a merciful God and that you love us so. Please forgive me for my judgments and for my angry thoughts. I am truly sorry for offending you because of my doubt. I love you, Father, and I know you will show me the way. Guide me to the path of healing, and give me courage to be more obedient to your teachings of love and kindness. You blessed us with forgiveness through your perfect Son, and I thank you for His perfect sacrifice, which saved us from our iniquity. I love you, Lord, and I really need you now. Please be with me. Amen.

Ailments

My eyes are blinded from the anger I have
for not knowing your despair.
My ears keep ringing with the news that you are really gone.
My nose keeps sniffing and tears keep flowing
for the hope you could not find.
My voice keeps hitching whenever I speak your name.
My shoulders are so heavy from the burden of how you left me.
My heart aches with such pain for my loss of your company.
My lungs are so tight with the uncertainty of your whereabouts.
My legs cannot carry the weight of my cross.
My soul keeps praying you find the faith that you lost.
Lord, please heal me, please comfort me, please ease my pain.

You also be patient Establish your hearts, for the coming of the Lord is at hand. Do not grumble, brethren, against one another, that you may not be judged; behold, the Judge is standing at the doors. (James 5:8, 9)

Let Me Go

Pray for me and let me go.
I don't want you to cry.
My mistake is mine alone.
Stop asking the question "Why?"
I know you must be angry
And furious at me
For leaving you to live your life
And wonder endlessly.
I couldn't tell you how I felt
Or give you any sign.
Just believe you're not at fault,
All the blame is mine.
Forgive me for my selfishness.
Please forgive me for the hurt.
I know you were surprised by this.
I gave no cause for alert.
Just let me go and live in peace
So I can make amends.
For only God can heal my soul
And make my suffering end.

More than that, we rejoice in our sufferings, knowing that suffering produces endurance, and endurance produces character, and character produces hope, and hope does not disappoint us, because God's love has been poured into our hearts through the Holy Spirit who has been given to us. (Romans 5:3–5)

Spread Hope

I am the whisper in the wind, the humming in your ear.
I am the sun that warms your skin, the breeze that blows your hair.
I am the hope in clouds of gray, that silver lining glow.
I am the pink in the setting sun's ray, the stream in nature's flow.
Believe that I surround you now in different shape and form,
And if you're asking "why" and "how,"
God saved me from the storm.
His great mercy released me, but he gave me a task to do.
To show the beauty of His charity and
spread His hope through you.

Suicide—how can anything positive come out of such a trag-edy? Those who survive are left heartbroken and ashamed. Any death is hard to deal with, but suicide always leaves us with a sense of fail-ure. We worry for the soul, and we are left with moral dilemmas and questioning our faith. We deal with guilt and often place blame. Faith is hard-won because we wonder how God could let a person become so despondent as to take their own life. God gives us freewill. Therefore, it is our choice to believe in the *divine*, in *love*, in God.

Eternal God, in whom mercy is endless and the treasury of compas-sion inexhaustible, look kindly upon and increase your mercy in us that in difficult moments, we might not despair nor become despondent, but with great confidence, submit ourselves to Your holy will, which is love and mercy itself. Amen.

The truth is that we look at this misfortune with judgment in our eyes. We judge those who took their lives. We judge those around them for not noticing their intentions. We judge ourselves for not doing something more to save them. Guilt does not come from the Lord; it comes from our disobedience in what Jesus Christ taught us: how to love one another.

We are only human, and our judgments are imperfect and unfair. We will be judged in the same manner as we judge others, but to be nonjudgmental is to understand that everyone is tempted and everyone makes mistakes. We don't know what's really in the minds of others; we only know what they communicate to us. We feel that we have the right to be angry, to hold a grudge, to be unforgiving. But love gives us the divine right to forgive, to release, to give it to God.

> For God so loved the world that he gave his only begotten Son, that whoever believes in him should not perish but have eternal life. (John 3:16)

Remember how mighty our Creator is? With forgiveness in our hearts, God will take care of everything. The Lord has mercy for those who ask for forgiveness, and through His merciful love, we are freed from the chains of our anger when we forgive. Forgiveness frees us from the burden of guilt and gives us a different cross to bear. Christ Jesus carried the cross of our sins to Calvary and gave us a cross of love to bear, so in all things, we must be gentle, kind, and loving, even through the anger, the pain, the suffering.

Forgiveness is such a powerful tool in reaching that beautiful goal of peace. It frees us from the pain and turmoil caused by our grievances, and it grants us serenity to accept our circumstances. We have the right to have peace of mind, especially in times of suffering. We have no control over the actions or thoughts of another human being. That's not our right, but it is okay to forgive ourselves for not being able to "save" them. We can only advise or give guidance and hope the influence we make is positive. Forgiveness opens the door for love to enter and to be spread from our hearts. To forgive is to be forgiven. In the Lord's Prayer, Jesus said we are forgiven as we forgive others.

> Then he adds, "I will remember their sins and their misdeeds no more." Where there is forgiveness of these, there is no longer any offering for sin. (Hebrews 10:17–18)

If there is anything positive that comes out of the tragedy of suicide, it is humility, forgiveness, compassion, greater appreciation for life, an understanding that we are not alone and opens a path to a deeper faith. We cannot get over something like this without being kind and considerate to one another. We have to be humble, because we don't know the answers, and we have to forgive in order to move forward. In such situations, we tend to talk to God more and lean on the promises of Christ with a more personal connection, so we need faith. Forgiveness frees us from our grief, and we can then let God deal with the one who has caused that grief.

We are all children of God, and as brothers and sisters in Christ, we must guide one another with unconditional love back to the Lord. Strength comes from the Lord and the power of his might. With this knowledge, we see Him and open our eyes to the light of His Son; it shines as bright as the sun. We have to trust that God will take care of us, and we have to let Him take the lead, especially when we are in mourning and dealing with suicide.

> Hear my cry, O God, listen to my prayer; from the end of the earth I call to you, when my heart is faint. Lead to the rock that is higher than I; for you are my refuge, a strong tower against the enemy. Let me dwell in your tent for ever! Oh, to be safe under the shelter of your wings. (Psalms 61:1–4)

Through Your Storm

If you're feeling down and lost, and all your hope is gone…
Know that you were worth a life: the Holy Father's Son.
A perfect sacrifice was made because He loved us so.
Just turn to Him for guidance when you're really sad and low.
I will be praying for you and those who feel torn
That God will let you see He's there to
guide you through your storm.

What I See

I couldn't see perfection in the person in my mirror,
Not even a reflection of the light divine that's pure.
I couldn't see the gifts that people claimed I had.
All I saw were rifts and failures of my pride.
I tried to see the image of God staring back into my eyes.
Instead I saw a message that I was unworthy and unwise.
Then I read the Word, and it brought me back to love.
God's voice I clearly heard coming loudly from above.
That I was made as I should be for the purpose only God could see.
And now my eyes are vividly opened to love as they should be.
I now see in the mirror the divine inside of me
And understand my purpose is to be the perfect me.

Each of us is created with a higher and perfect good. Impatience never gives anything "good or great" a chance to work. Patience, on the other hand, allows a person to see potential in every situation, to see the possible in the impossible, and it allows compassion and understanding to come into play. We have to be patient in our desperate moments, because our feelings can blind us to what is right. When we are hurting, we can do insurmountable damage to the relationships that are healthy for us. Therefore, we have to trust that the Lord will carry us through, and we have to let Him take over. Nothing can separate us from the love of Christ, except us.

I know a woman that went to visit her daughter's grave site every day for two years after her daughter committed suicide. One day she asked me what I thought about it, because a lot of her friends and family discouraged her from going to the cemetery. They told her it was unhealthy and that her mourning would hold her daughter's spirit back. I asked her what she did when she went to the grave site, and she told me she goes there to pray for her daughter. The grave site is the place where she felt most comfortable to pray for her daughter. I understood that perfectly! She didn't go there out of self-pity or out of sorrow; she went there to save her daughter's life, her afterlife. I think it is completely in God's hands, and I know He loves us, but I was astounded by her devotion to save the soul of her much-loved daughter. It reminded me of Saint Monica of Hippo, who prayed for her son Augustine, who later became a saint himself. My response to her was that I would keep praying for her daughter as well, and that if she needed to visit the cemetery every day to pray that the Father will take care of her daughter, then she should continue to do it for as long as she wanted. She was praying out of love and concern; she wasn't drowning in her sorrow for the loss of her daughter. There is a big difference between unconditional love and self-indulgence.

> But if any one has caused pain, he has caused it not to me, but in some measure-not to put it too severely-to you all. For such a one this punishment by the majority is enough; so you should rather turn to forgive and comfort him, or he may be overwhelmed by excessive sorrow. So I beg you to reaffirm your love for him. For this is why I wrote, that I might test you and know whether you are obedient in everything. Any one whom you forgive, I also forgive. What I have forgiven, if I have forgiven anything, has been for your sake in the presence of Christ, to keep Satan from gaining the advantage over us; for we are not ignorant of his designs. (2 Corinthians 2:5–11)

The grieving mother's actions were unselfish acts of love. I think the soul hears us when it leaves our bodies. It can hear our crying, and it can hear our prayers. We are all connected. If we weep out of sorrow, who is it for? If you hear someone crying because of something you've done, wouldn't you feel guilt and regret? Guilt does not make a person change or heal; it makes them feel unworthy. When we pray for the dead, they know we love them. Shouldn't we commend their spirits into God's hands, where they belong and where they can have peace? When we pray for those who have mistakenly taken their lives, our prayers appeal to God's mercy, which is love in action. Our love is a reflection of the love our dearly departed has given us during their life. They will see their lives, they will see they were loved, and they will have a chance to turn to God and ask for forgiveness. Remember, being Catholic, I believe in purgatory and the purification of our souls to enter the kingdom of heaven. Also, our Father hears our pleas, and He answers them according to His will. The spirit of our loved ones can rise again, because of our loving prayers for them and His loving answers. He is the only judge that is just, and we should leave it all up to Him.

> For if he were not expecting that those who had fallen would rise again, it would have been superfluous and foolish to pray for the dead. But if he was looking to the splendid reward that is laid up for those who fall asleep in godliness, it was a holy and pious thought. Therefore he made atonement for the dead, that they might be delivered from their sin. (2 Maccabees 12:44–45)

In the flesh, we desire many things we do not need. Sometimes we want those things because we think they will make a big difference in the quality of our lives, somehow make it better, somehow fulfill our needs. People are tempted by so many desires: an easier life, luxurious things, better companions, vanity, superiority, and the like, but we are blinded by our feelings: envy, lust, anger, and pride. The riches of this world spoil us, and it is so easy to get caught up in its hype.

These worldly endeavors are enticing but, in truth, are temporary and become empty. Once we reach these goals, we want something else because they are satisfactory only for a time and no longer offer challenge or appeal. We can get stuck in this pattern.

We tend to forget that God has sovereignty. God has a plan for us, and it is up to us to trust, accept, and follow the path He has laid out for us. God guides us through our souls. When we find something we are passionate about and experience all the fruit of the Spirit in that pursuit, our heart's desire will be met. This is God's plan for our lives. The Spirit gives us what we need to follow this path, and it is an easy road once taken.

All of our natural gifts and talents support us in the work God has put us here for. Gifts of the Holy Spirit are granted us when we decide to follow God's path, and these gifts are called charisms. When the Holy Spirit starts working through us, we accomplish a great work in the world that affects the whole of mankind. We are all made to do things with great love. That love is the catechist of good.

You Took the Time

When you took the time to hear my thoughts,
You never really knew
That you saved me from a pit I was falling in.
Then you held me close and held me tight.
I knew your love was strong and true.
Hope shined through, and faith showed up to win.
You smiled when you listened to me.
Then you said things could be fine,
And I heard the wisdom ring from your sweet voice.
Just your time had saved me,
And I'm glad you saw the sign,
For I never really knew I had a choice.

This world is not a peaceful place, not a kind place, and this world is not full of love, but God's love is unfailing and beyond understanding. We can be the venue in which God shows the world love. I've found that the only thing that has ever made a significant difference in my life is turning to Jesus, praying to our Father, trusting His plan for me, and asking the Holy Spirit to guide me.

My heart and my prayers go out to the families affected by suicide, most especially, for those who've passed on. I must say that we may never know the answer to the question "Why?" but peace will come with a walk of faith in God. May the peace and love of Christ be with you all. St. Francis of Assisi often said that everything he did, he did "for the love of Christ."

> Trust in the Lord with all your heart, and do not rely on your own insight. In all your ways acknowledge him, and he will make straight your paths. (Proverbs 3:5–6)

> Why, we felt that we had received the sentence of death; but that was to make us rely not on ourselves but on God who raises the dead; he delivered us from so deadly a peril, and he will deliver us; on him we have set our hope that he will deliver us again. You also must help us by prayer, so that many will give thanks on our behalf for the blessing granted us in answer to many prayers. (2 Corinthians 1:9–11)

Some days a person feels less than what they are really worth. What are we really worth? The truth is that we are worth more than anything this physical world can offer! We are worth the divine mercy and love of God! God breathed life into us and loves us.

The Holy Spirit is with us and has never left. Who are we to say we are unworthy of something we can't understand? If we are made in the image of God, then we are worthy of every part of creation—we are part of *creation*! We are a beautiful and perfect work of art, cherished and inspired straight from God's love. Christ was an example of perfect love.

The *passion of the cross* is a journey in the anguish of life and an example of fortitude in faith. Faith keeps our focus on God, and God is *love*. Therefore, I feel in my heart that the Lord brings us back to Him regardless of our mistakes. God loves us no matter what, and nothing is impossible with God.

Those who have passed on need prayers, not grief, not longing, not sadness. They need to hear our voices rise in prayer and in love so they can feel the mercy in our souls. Mercy is love in action, and prayer is an act of love! The power of our voice is strong. It can do so much to accomplish the tasks set before us. It can encourage and promote, it can energize and ignite, it can save! Be truthful in your heart and believe in the words you speak, because they affect whomever you are speaking to, whether it is the living or the dead.

> I have seen his ways, but I will heal him; I will lead him and repay him with comfort, creating for his mourners the fruit of the lips. Peace, peace, to the far and to the near, says the Lord; and I will heal him. (Isaiah 57:18–19)

Sometimes the joy in life hides its face in the shadows of pride, but if you drop the armor that hides the sun, the Son will surely shine His light and help you find your joy. I bring up pride because pride can prevent healing in so many ways. When pride comes into play, we fail to humble ourselves before the Lord and others. We try to handle our grievances on our own, but instead, our anger feeds the fire and festers inside us. Pride prevents us from saying we're sorry or that we forgive. It makes us think that if we forgive those who've offended us, we will look like fools.

The opposite is true, because God forgives us as we forgive. Pride also keeps us from showing compassion and empathy toward the dead and keeps us from prayer. We have the power to save, but pride puts us first and others last. We have the authority to give hope to others, but pride keeps us from leaving our comfort zones. Pride can be a reservoir of sin (that which leads us away from God), so we must set it aside if we want to find peace.

My Pride

I could not drop the mask that everybody sees,
But in my battle, the enemy finally brought me to my knees.
A strong and willful soldier where no weakness could reside,
I didn't know the reservoir of sin would be my pride.
I should have opened up my heart and let you see my pain,
But the armor that I always wore made me leave in vain.
I know I never said goodbye and went away in haste.

I should have endured so hope could shine
through; instead, it lay in waste.
I've always thought that knowledge would help me to defeat
The enemy inside my heart, but he laid me at his feet.
He tricked me into believing that I knew it would be best
To escape the cross I bear in life and find eternal rest.
Regretfully, I know now it is always better to live
And ask of you to love me still, and most of all to forgive.
I love you, and I'm sorry for the tears you shed for me,
But now it's in our Father's hands, and I pray He sets me free.

I am going to summarize my Catholic and cultural tradition once again, because, in every loss of life, this community in God has helped me heal. It is the Catholic and cultural custom to say the rosary for nine days after a loved one passes on. We gather and pray together for the family and the souls of our dearly departed. Through this custom, I've learned that the preparation, in itself, during these nine days is a path to healing. In my experience, this time has helped me because my mind was focused on the repetitive tasks of preparing for the guests and prevented me from feeling sorry for my own loss. During the gatherings, friends, relatives, and acquaintances would share their stories about my loved one's past, and those stories kept him or her alive in my heart and mind. They also surprised me and showed me that you don't always know someone completely. You can still learn about them when they've passed on, so that means to me that their spirit is still very active. You also see your support group. People come and offer their help even if you don't know them. Love shows. Self-pity often suppresses the healing, because you cannot hear what people say or see what is going on around you when you focus on the death or the end. When the rosaries end and the people stop coming, the grief comes, but we've been strengthened and are prepared. God is always present, and if you focus on Him first, He has you wrapped in His arms to comfort and protect you, to give you strength, and to fortify you.

I've been to many funerals, many not Catholic services, but love is always present in the hearts of those gathering. I am not an authority of religion, and I don't care about religion in the general sense, but in the light of death, love shines very brightly. I believe in faith and love. I have just been very lucky that those around me were faithful as well.

> I therefore, a prisoner for the Lord, beg
> you to walk in a manner worthy of the calling to
> which you have been called, with all lowliness and
> meekness, with patience, forbearing one another
> in love, eager to maintain the unity of the Spirit
> in the bond of peace. (Ephesians 4:1–3)

I urge you to be aware of the people around you who are trying to disappear. Make it known that everyone counts, and let your loved ones know they are important and are thought of even if it doesn't seem like it. Hope lies in the heart of each of us, so let everyone you know believe in them. Life is worth the fight, and any problem can be solved if we have faith, hope, and love. Let them know that the Lord will answer their questions if they have the faith to ask Him. Let them know that our Father will take care of us if we put our lives in His hands.

It is so much easier to know what our bodies need: food when we're hungry, drink when we're thirsty, aspirin for a headache, and so on. But when our souls are in need of something, it is much harder to tell. When that empty feeling or loneliness hits us deep inside and we don't know what to do, we should *pray*, with all our heart, that God will show us the way and grant us a reprieve from our sorrow or anxiety.

> Likewise the Spirit helps us in our weakness;
> for we do not know how to pray as we ought, but
> the Spirit himself intercedes for us with sighs too
> deep for words. (Romans 8:26)

Part 6

The Dawn

Let no one ever come to you without leaving better and happier. Be the living expression of God's kindness: kindness in your face, kindness in your eyes, kindness in your smile. (St. Teresa of Calcutta)

Poet's Heart

I am a fool with a poet's heart
With soulful thoughts made into art.
A sense of passion in my words
Changing dreams into visions heard.
Foolhardy though I know it sounds
From deep within my heartbeat pounds
With love's desires calling forth
To bring about its fruitful birth.

Healing is the main reason I write, and love is the reason I will continue to write. The dawn is morning's first light. I want you to know that you have a right to move on. In my darkness, I found the divine, and in the divine, I found the light, and the light is me. St. Catherine of Sienna said, "Be who God intended you to be and you will set the world on fire." I believe that each of us is a beautiful and perfect gift to others. We are all called to be saints. When we accept the gifts and talents that are true to our making, we can set the world on fire with God's *sacred love*. This is holiness.

We are valuable and important, and we matter. Make those ripples in the world that can only come from you. You are unique and you are special. There is no other person in the world exactly like you, because you are meant to make an impact in your own exclusive way according to God's plan for your life.

Do not fear the world and all it encompasses, because God has given you exactly what you need to live the life that was intended for you. Be true to your calling, and be true to the unselfish desires of your heart. They are usually in compliance with God's plan. And trust in the divine. Listen to the voices within, and your path will be made clear, and that path is perfect. You are the light of the world, and this is the dawn.

My Dream Today

I want to share my hopes and dreams,
But sometimes no one cares it seems.
We're caught up in our daily tasks,
Then wonder how the time has passed.
Dreams must be nurtured, and hope must be shared
So we can look forward to a life that's revered.
And just as the sun shines every day,
I pray God's sweet grace will shine your way.
I wish the day brings joy and peace
And several happy memories.
My goal today is to show my style
And to spark some hope with a friendly smile.
Who knows? It might ignite a dream
In someone who is suffering.

Hope

Sometimes people pass the day without a glimmer of light,
So do your part and show someone the hope that lies inside.
Some kindness to a stranger, some laughter with a friend,

There is no end to the power each of us holds within.
You have a chance to heal someone who is laden with a burden.
Just show the care and love you have by
leaving your arms and heart open.

The Lord speaks through deeds of faith and acts of love. Be His voice! Kind words always build a person up and give hope and confidence that things will be okay. They help to heal grief and anxiety. Nothing bad comes from kindness if it is done in the name of love. We must be loving in our works, peaceful in our thoughts, and kind in our hearts. Show compassion to those who are less fortunate and empathy for those in pain.

Make your ripples of love spread around you, and repeat the ripples of love that were passed to you from your dearly departed. Let their love ebb and flow throughout the world, and never let it end with you.

Beauty is in the eyes of the beholder, so isn't it true that beauty is also in the eye of our creator? We are beautiful, and we are perfectly made. God loves us so much, and each of us is made special in His eyes. Never lose faith that God, the Father, cares for you because He saved us all through His Son. Know the Father through the Son in and with the Holy Spirit.

Humility makes all the kindness that comes our way like blessings from heaven. More often than not, pride and ambition blind us to the beauty that surrounds us now. Pride comes before the fall, so it's better to be humble than to be humbled. James 4:6 reminds us, "God is opposed to the proud, but gives grace to the humble." I might sound like I'm preaching, but I've learned so much through this journey.

I know that time is quick. We rejoice in life, but time is short. I've wasted much of my life making choices that taught lessons that brought me right back to where I was supposed to be in the first place. I've learned to trust God, and in turn, God has entrusted a beautiful adventure to me.

I pray that all the lessons in your life brings you closer to divine love and care of your neighbor. Love yourself, because God has made you perfect in His perfect plan. You are valuable and of more worth than you can ever imagine. I pray for your healing, and God bless you.

The Rain

Every day has been a gift with all its joys and sorrows. With every raincloud, beauty follows, and I embrace, wholeheartedly, the rain and the rainbow. My life is beautiful!

Love Is the Key

Hatred, despair, and dependency lock the doors to a wealth of happiness.
Love is the key to prosperity.

Loving yourself
- Opens the door of confidence and leads you to success in your endeavors.
- Opens the door of honesty and allows you to face yourself and deal with the trials of your life.
- Opens the door of peace and allows you to be content with the choices you make.
- Opens the door of hope and allows you to reach for your dreams.
- Opens the door of faith and help you to believe that you are special.
- Opens the door of forgiveness and allows you to deal with the world around you.
- Opens the door of mercy and allows you to be caring.
- Opens the door to compassion and allows you to be empathetic to others in pain.
- Opens the door to others.

Loving others
- Opens the door of acceptance and allows you to persevere in your ambitions.
- Opens the door of support and allows you to have a strong foundation of encouragement.
- Opens the door of understanding and allows you to see the truth in the eyes of your loved ones.
- Opens the door of trust and allows you to have helping hands when conquering your fears.
- Opens the door of respect and allows you to learn from their experience.
- Opens the door of companionship so you are not alone in times of trials.
- Opens the door of admiration and allows you to see the beauty inside each individual.
- Opens the door of friendship and teaches you about love.
- Opens the door to life.

Loving life
- Opens the door of excitement and allows you to move forward with anticipation.
- Opens the door of beauty and lets you see the wonder of God's glorious creation.
- Opens the door of patience and helps you see it is a virtue.
- Opens the door of adventure and helps you believe in miracles.
- Opens the door of hope and leads you to the place of dreams.
- Opens the door of faith and leads you to God.
- Loving God
- Opens the doors to everything.

God Will Help

Explore some new horizons.
Have faith in what you do.
Believe in all the things you are,
And God will help you through.
Take time for him alone to pray.
His light will shine your darkened way.
You'll find the safety in His gift
As He guides you through each busy day.
Try to make every moment full
As if it is your very last,
For like the light of a shooting star,
Life zooms by so fast.
Enjoy your life while there's still time.
Have faith in all you do.
Have hope and live your life with love,
And trust in the plan He has for you.
Hope in all that you can be.
Pray in all the things you do.
Be righteous in action and steadfast in love
And know God is always with you.

But he who does what is true comes to the light, that it may be clearly seen that his deeds have been wrought in God. (John 3:21)

Go out into the world today and love the people you meet. Let your presence light new light in the hearts of people. (St. Teresa of Calcutta)

When I say God is present in my life, I believe wholeheartedly that He is always with me. God is at the core of all I do. He is at the center of my marriage, He is at the forefront of every relationship I have, He is with me as I work, He is with me in play. He is with me in my joy and in my sorrow, dwelling in me, embracing my heart always. He is always part of my thoughts. I don't leave Him at church or in those places I feel most reverent. I move with God, because I know that God is my source. He is life!

Every day I ask Jesus to teach me how to love better, but walking in the way of Christ is difficult when there are worldly pursuits tugging all around. I want to be holy, and I want to walk among the saints. Only in union with the Spirit can we serve a mission of love with purity of heart. So I have to recommit and rededicate myself to that mission of love every single day, knowing that God is present even if He is silent or feels distant. I keep my heart in heaven, because I believe in eternity and in the promises of Christ. Therefore, in this life, I love.

I Long to Be

I long to be a light in the darkness…
to shine through the gloom and grant peace to your soul.
I long to be a spark in the timber…
to ignite the fires of ambition and goals.
I long to be a giver of hope…
to vanquish despair and make burdens light.
I long to teach love…
with kindness and strength, unconditional and pure,
…and a great deal of faith.

My Legacy

The beauty of my life lies within the twinkling eyes
that look upon me with hope and trust. The
glory of my life is held within the hearts I touch with
unbound love and undying faith. My legacy will be
the seeds of friendship and generosity I will plant.

For This Beauty

The bluest sky I've ever seen
Surrounding me are fields of green
With flowers blooming everywhere,
A sight no other can compare.
The treetops seem to touch the sky.
The birds in V formation fly.
The clouds have silver lining too.
For this beauty, Lord, thank you.

Take Me to a Place

Take me to a place…
…where beauty is in every shape and form.
…where the flowers bloom in vivid colors.
…where the sounds are children's laughter,
    bird's song, and gossip's chatter.
…where the scents are sweet and the music
    of the place just fills your soul.
…where my mind can wander and my heart is full.
…where I can speak freely about something or about nothing.
…where hope is created and dreams are reachable.
Take me home.

We are made for each other, and we can influence others by our care. Be a good role model. Be thankful for the role models in your life, because they have been a blessing to you from God.

People are often unreasonable and self-centered.
Forgive them anyway.
If you are kind, people may accuse you of ulterior motives.
Be kind anyway.
If you are honest, people may cheat you.
Be honest anyway.
If you find happiness, people may be jealous.

Be happy anyway.
The good you do today may be forgotten tomorrow.
Do good anyway.
Give the world the best you have and it may never be enough.
Give your best anyway.
For you see, in the end, it is between you and God.
It was never between you and them anyway.
(St. Teresa of Calcutta)

Love may come easy to some, but unconditional love takes devotion and sincerity of the heart. It is patient, kind, humble, joyful, peaceful, faithful, self-controlled, and good. These are all fruit of the spirit, and they are the most beautiful and lasting gifts anyone could ever receive. They take a lot of work and cannot be accomplished without the help of the Holy Spirit. You should know that it takes kindness and humility to get our points across, it takes faith to know that you will be pardoned for any offenses, and it takes joy and peace to remain sane and caring. We have to be submissive and gentle to those we care for, and sometimes it takes a lifetime to learn.

My Tree

There is a tree that depicts everyone's life. Every branch that grows is a chapter we have lived through. It may have been short, long, weak, or strong, but we made it. Every leaf that appears is an experience we have had whether it is good or bad; the more you have, the more full and beautiful your tree. Every flower is an opportunity to make connections and bring joy. Every fruit it bears is a gift we've given to others, from just a smile or hello to the ultimate gift of unconditional love. Every fallen leaf, every fallen flower, and every fallen fruit becomes mulch to enhance the foundation of our lives. Strive to make your tree full and fruitful. Mine has become an orchard and the fruits of our lives are plentiful.

Pleasures

Life is full of simple pleasures.
All around us little treasures.
Beauty seen through eager eyes,
Stories that make us laugh and cry,
Joyful laughter and bright gay cheer,
Exciting moments that come year after year.
Delectable smells of something baking,
Delicious food prepared for the taking.
God makes our lives like the rarest jewel,
Each unique and wonderful.

Not all of us can do great things, but we can do small things with great love. (St. Teresa of Calcutta)

Light

Gray clouds hiding bluer skies
Surrounding me with wet and gloom,
But within, my soul survives.
A light so eager to illume.
A light of hope beyond despair,
A light of peace in nameless wrath,
A light of faith in worldly fear,
A light of love that shines the path.
A pure love with joy so great
That wants to shine without control
On people led to me by fate
To heal the hearts of aching souls.

Blessed

I look outside my window, and there are colors everywhere!
Different shades of green and yellow,
Red splashes here and there.
Such beauty penetrates my heart and shows my Lord loves me,
For He allows the joy of earth to shine quite vividly.
He blessed my eyes to see in awe the wonders of the world.
He blessed my ears to hear the songs of wind and tree and bird.
The happiness I feel from earth is pure and unseen.
A place to cherish and preserve with love,
His majesty pristine.

Life is so short. Our time on earth is only an instant in the scope of eternity, and in that short moment, we make such an impact on everything that surrounds us. Life, like a twenty-four-hour cycle, can be reflected in the process of a day. The sun shines, and we live in the warmth and the light of its glow. The sun sets, and we search for rest and safety in the loss of light and the coolness of the night. We find rest, and then we are refreshed to begin again. Life is the daytime, death is the nighttime, and dawn is the hope of life eternal.

During the day, we strive to accomplish the tasks and goals we set for ourselves. We manage our time so that we can complete our duties before the day ends and prepare for when night falls. We make connections with those around us and build relationships that teach us how different and how special each individual is. We give, we take, we laugh, and we share. What happens when there are not enough hours in the day and the twilight comes before our work is through? Dusk arrives and the darkness falls. We can no longer accomplish that which can only be finished in the daylight. We are out of time.

Our life on earth is our day, death is our night, and hope is our dawn. Every person I have met has determined how bright my days, my life, have been because we make lasting impressions on those around us every day. By the same token, my effect on a relative, friend, or acquaintance will determine the darkness of my nights. Did I love them well enough in the time I was given to share with them?

There should be no regrets! There should be no regrets for not spending as much time with our loved ones, as long as the moments we shared with them were memorable and loving. There should be no regrets for not reaching the goals we set for ourselves if we attempted, wholeheartedly and with passion, to reach them. If we practice patience, gentleness, self-control, and love in all we do, then regret will have no place to perch its nasty talons. Instead, we should celebrate the daylight accomplishments and rejoice in the relationships we have had. We should celebrate the valleys we've forged, the bridges we've crossed, the talents we've perfected, the gifts of the day. The warmth and love of friendship are the ties that bind us together. The connections and achievements we make during the daylight hours leave behind a portion of our goodness. In the darkness and coolness of the night, we should rejoice and remember. Shine on!

> I alone cannot change the world, but I can cast a stone across the waters to create many ripples. (St. Teresa of Calcutta)

What Ripple Will You Make?

What ripple will you make?
Would it go beyond your gate?
Or will it be a strong one that can surpass a certain state?
Will your ripple be destructive, or will it build up better traits?
Will it be an example of pure love and ripple beyond hate?
What ripple will you make?

> "Teacher, which is the great commandment in the law?" And he said to him, "You shall love the Lord your God with all your heart, and with all your soul, and with all your mind. This is the great and first commandment. And a second is like it, you shall love your neighbor as yourself. On these two commandments depend all the law and the prophets. (Matthew 22:36–40)

About the Author

 R. B. Craven was born Ruth Garrido Blas in Guam, USA, in an atmosphere of strong cultural and spiritual beliefs. Even as a young woman, she knew the importance of incorporating her faith in all that she did, and she knew that she would want to use her life to affect the lives of others. Realizing her ability to understand and care for others, she became a caregiver. After high school, she pursued a career in early childhood education and was successful in encouraging others to use their abilities for the good of the world. Later, she worked with adults disabled with physical and mental disorders. She also worked with the elderly, many in hospice. This experience humbled her and gave her a new outlook. She now volunteers to assist senior citizens in all aspects of their lives. Writing poetry and journaling were always a part of her makeup, as was her desire that through these she would spread kindness.

CPSIA information can be obtained
at www.ICGtesting.com
Printed in the USA
BVHW032239070321
601886BV00003B/17